VAMPIRES

VAMPIRES

Emotional Predators Who Want to Suck the Life Out of You

by

Daniel Rhodes

and

Dr. Kathleen Rhodes

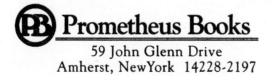

Prometheus Books

59 John Glenn Drive
Amherst, NewYork 14228-2197

Published 1998 by Prometheus Books

02 01 00 99 98   5 4 3 2 1

Library of Congress Cataloging-in-Publication Data

Rhodes, Daniel.
    Vampires : emotional predators who want to suck the life out of you / by
Daniel Rhodes and Kathleen Rhodes.
        p.   cm.
    Includes bibliographical references and index.
    ISBN 1–57392–191–2 (cloth : alk. paper)
    1. Interpersonal conflict. 2. Interpersonal relations. 3. Vampires,
Miscellanea. I. Rhodes, Kathleen, Dr. II. Title.
BF637.I48R48   1998
158.2—dc21   97–39228
                                                                  CIP

Printed in the United States of America on acid-free paper

This book is dedicated to real heroes, who do the hard work, often underpaid and unappreciated, that keeps the world running.

Special thanks to our story contributors, who offered their personal experiences with emotional vampirism.

To Frances Kuffel, on many levels, especially her insights into *Dracula*.

And to Kim and Dan, who carried us.

The bed in that old chamber is occupied. A creature formed in all fashions of loveliness lies in a half sleep upon that ancient couch— a girl young and beautiful as a spring morning. Her long hair has escaped from its confinement and streams over the blackened coverings of the bedstead; she has been restless in her sleep, for the clothing of the bed is in much confusion. One arm is over her head, the other hangs nearly off the side of the bed near to which she lies. A neck and bosom that would have formed a study for the rarest sculptor that ever Providence gave genius to, were half disclosed. She moaned slightly in her sleep . . .

A tall figure is standing on the ledge immediately outside the long window. It is its finger-nails upon the glass that produces the sound so like the hail, now that the hail has ceased. Intense fear paralysed the limbs of that beautiful girl. That one shriek is all she can utter—with hands clasped, a face of marble, a heart beating so wildly in her bosom, that each moment it seems as if it would break its confines, eyes distended and fixed upon the window, she waits, froze with horror. The pattering and clattering of the nails continue. No word is spoken, and now she fancies she can trace the darker form of that figure against the window, and she can see the long arms moving to and fro, feeling for some mode of entrance . . . She tries to scream again but a choking sensation comes over her, and she cannot. It is too dreadful—she tries to move—each limb seems weighed down by tons of lead—she can but in a hoarse faint whisper cry,—

"Help—help—help—help!" . . .

The figure turns half round, and the light falls upon the face. It is perfectly white—perfectly bloodless. The eyes look like polished tin; the lips are drawn back, and the principal feature next to those dreadful eyes is the teeth—the fearful-looking teeth—projecting like those of some wild animal, hideously, glaringly white, and fang-like. It approaches the bed with a strange, gliding movement. It clashes together the long nails that literally appear to hang from the finger ends. No sound comes from its lips. Is she going mad— that young and beautiful girl exposed to so much terror? she has drawn up all her limbs; she cannot even now say help . . .

With a sudden rush that could not be foreseen—with a strange howling cry that was enough to awaken terror in every breast, the figure seized the long tresses of her hair, and twining them round his bony hands he held her to the bed. Then she screamed—Heaven granted her the power to scream. Shriek followed shriek in rapid succession. The bed-clothes fell in a heap by the side of the bed—she was dragged by her long silken hair completely on to it again. Her beautifully rounded limbs quivered with the agony of her soul. The glassy, horrible eyes of the figure ran over that angelic form with a hideous satisfaction—horrible profanation. He drags her head to the bed's edge. He forces it back by the long hair still entwined in his grasp. With a plunge he seizes her neck in his fang-like teeth— a gush of blood, and a hideous sucking noise follows. The girl has swooned, and the vampire is at his hideous repast!

James Malcolm Rymer, *Varney the Vampyre,*
or, The Feast of Blood (1845)

Pronounced mental inhibition and depression quickly come on. The patient feels herself without interest, incapable of pleasure, unspeakably unhappy, and tired of life. Life seems to her a heavy burden, and it pains her to think that she has become indifferent to her duties as mother and housewife. But she is also incapable of ful-

filling them. She is devoid of energy, depressed, incapable of any activity, fatigued, and exhausted, especially in the morning after she has passed a sleepless night. She has the complete despairing sense of her disease and of her mental incapability. For months at a time she does not sleep and she is forced to take chloral hydrate {a sedative}. She is tortured with thoughts that she will never get well, and longs for death as a deliverance. Occasionally there are reactive outbreaks of despair, which then end in an outburst of weeping.

She is without appetite, but must force herself to eat, feels over-satiated, and a distressing dryness in her throat. Almost all the time the patient suffers with a distressing feeling of pressure in the back of the head, numbness in the hands, pressure in the feet, and pain along the inner surface of the thighs.

Suddenly one day the painful condition disappears. She sleeps again, has appetite, takes pleasure, and feels more than happy, though this feeling of deliverance from the disease cannot be regarded as a maniacal, final stage. At least, at this time she becomes again a very intelligent woman, and is regarded as such by her family. Now the body-weight increases rapidly, which in the beginning of the attack sank rapidly and which during the whole of the attack remained at not more than 59 to 61 kilograms, until her normal weight of about 70 kilograms is attained. During the intervals the patient is physically and mentally well, only she is now and then distressed by the thought that the fatal disturbance may sooner or later come on again.

The last attack, which is described in a letter dated toward the end of March, 1881, was protracted, owing to the fact that at the time of the presumed termination of it her father (April 1880) and other members of the family died. . . . [emphasis added]

Richard Von Krafft-Ebing, *Text-Book of Insanity* (1905)

Contents

At our last meeting, we considered the healthy-minded temperament, the temperament which has a constitutional incapacity for prolonged suffering, and in which the tendency to see things optimistically is like a water of crystallization in which the individual's character is set. We saw how this temperament may become the basis for a peculiar type of religion, a religion in which the good, even the good of this world's life, is regarded as the essential thing for a rational being to attend to. This religion directs him to settle his scores with the more evil aspects of the universe by systematically declining to lay them to heart or make much of them, by ignoring them in his reflective calculations, or even, on occasion, by denying outright that they exist. Evil is a disease; and worry over disease is itself an additional form of disease, which only adds to the original complaint . . .

Let us now say good-by for a while to all this way of thinking, and turn towards those persons who cannot so swiftly throw off the burden of the consciousness of evil, but are congenitally fated to suffer from its presence . . .

In the healthiest and most prosperous existence, how many links of illness, danger, and disaster are always interposed? Unsuspectedly from the bottom of every fountain of pleasure, as the old poet said, something bitter rises up: a touch of nausea, a falling dead of the delight, a whiff of melancholy, things that sound a knell, for fugitive as they may be, they bring a feeling of coming from a deeper region and often have an appalling convincingness. The buzz of life ceases at their touch as a piano-string stops sounding when the damper falls upon it . . .

Failure, then, failure! So the world stamps us at every turn. We strew it with our blunders, our misdeeds, our lost opportunities, with all the memorials of our inadequacy to our vocation. And with what a damning emphasis does it then blot us out! No easy fine, no mere apology or formal expiation, will satisfy the world's demands, but every pound of flesh exacted is soaked with all its blood.

William James, *The Varieties of Religious Experience* (1902)

Introduction

AFRAID OF THE DARK

Daniel Rhodes

I saw my first Dracula movie when I was nine, with a bunch of other kids on a treat for somebody's birthday. It was one of the old Hammer flicks, loaded with campy melodrama and technicolor blood that looked redder than real, and it was my first exposure to what are still some of the scariest scenes in film:

Dracula, appearing at dusk like a bat from his lair and creeping *headfirst* down the castle wall; the vampire brides about to "kiss" Jonathan Harker, until Dracula tears them away, then throws them a still-squirming sack to appease their rage; the agonized mother

15

shrieking for her child at the castle gate—until the howling of wolves draws close; the fiend rising, rigid, from his coffin to pursue the last frantic sailor on the doomed ship—

And of course, the nightgowned heroine lying wide-eyed, breast heaving, while the sinister black figure stalks across the room, and with a sweep of his cape, bends over her soft throat.

For the next week, I absolutely refused to be alone after sundown, and in my heart of hearts, I'm still afraid of the dark.

Almost four decades have passed since then. I acquired a couple of college degrees, including one in psychology (although I'm no psychologist). I've spent a lot of time studying history, folklore and myth, religions, and esoteric philosophies (although I'm no scholar). I've done a fair amount of writing, and made it through lean times, which has been most of them, working construction.

Somewhere in there, I started to understand that the terror I had felt about vampires was not just the irrational reaction of a child.

VICTIMS

That realization came in a slow and roundabout way. I'll try to capsulize it.

Like most of us, I'm rarely affected directly by crime. But like most, I absorb my share of random hostility. It was never something I paid much attention to—until it started seeming that there was a lot more of it around. My daily life had gotten noticeably more difficult, in ways that were usually petty, and yet added up.

I realized I was angry, frustrated, sometimes afraid—not of crime or violence, but of something I couldn't quite grasp. More and more I heard friends, family, and even strangers expressing the same sentiment.

That, I suppose, was what started me on this track.

What first became clear is something that's apparent to everyone with their eyes open: our society is running amuck. This is happening on many fronts, but one in particular is basic: the erosion of personal responsibility, in the old-fashioned sense of decent treatment of others, and fairness in general.

Some forms of this are obvious. We're all familiar with the defense or nonpunishment of wrongdoers, both civil and criminal (often at huge public expense), via Kafka-esque legal wranglings. It's become a standard tactic that criminal defendants are themselves victims, of various societal and/or emotional pressures. If they happen to be wealthy, successful, privileged, this is not seen as a reason that they might be expected to find other methods, besides crime, to cope with problems. Instead, it only adds to their troubles in life.

Then there are news-making insurance settlements, where someone gets injured through his own carelessness and is awarded a huge sum on the grounds that he's a victim: a product manufacturer or watchdog should have foreseen the situation and gone to impossible lengths to prevent it.

Legitimate liability and workmen's compensation claims also get wildly inflated through "deep pockets" litigation, in which individuals and corporations with only the vaguest connections to the incident are included in lawsuits, on the grounds that they've contributed to the victim's injury. (It's a huge industry, with much of the money going to legal fees and taxes—and largely paid for by a general rise in insurance rates.)

A recent state supreme court decision seems perfectly in keeping. If a robber (or, presumably, rapist or murderer) breaks into your home, steals your firearm, and injures himself with it, he may successfully sue you. In this logic, it's your responsibility to prevent the theft. If you fail, it's your fault: he's a victim of your negligence.

More astonishing yet, there seems to be an increasing tendency to blame the *actual* victims of violent crime, for elicitation, or being in the wrong place at the wrong time, or simply having something someone else wanted.

Examples like those are extreme; I've oversimplified; and the reality has always differed from the fair-play ethic. But there's no doubt that there's been a radical change, over the past few decades, in the perception of what the individual owes to society, and vice versa. The someone-else-is-always-to-blame thinking—rarely overt, but oblique and under the surface—has become pervasive, trickling down, and up, from corporate and political arenas into the most common parts of everyday life. The trend continues to grow, with the message hammered home in countless ways.

This has many spin-offs. One is that the mentality blends easily into get-away-with-whatever-you-can. Another is that real victims, along with those who work to help and protect them, can get lost in the swamp.

This confusion between true victims and not-so-true ones is a point that kept cropping up, with increasing significance, through the writing of this book. We'll return to it.

BLOOD SCENT

For some time, I thought that that was all there was to the increase in low-level friction I was sensing. It comes as no surprise that in a no-fault society, aggressive behavior in general is on the upsurge.

But while I was wondering vaguely why the change had come about, and trying to figure out new ways to deal with it, another realization started flickering at the edges of my mental vision.

I wasn't looking for this. It came on its own.

Over the next years, mostly in that mysterious way our minds work without conscious direction, bits and pieces began to accumulate.

First, certain types of personal interactions drained my energy inordinately. These took two basic forms: normal contact with someone I knew—not argumentative or high-stress—which would leave me confused, fatigued, weakened; and encounters with strangers, where some minor brush, usually catching me by surprise, would turn quickly unpleasant. From these, I'd come away feeling shaken and angry. Both types were apparently random.

Second, on a closer look, many of these interactions were not random at all.

Third, identifiable characteristics and patterns began to appear.

When the surprise did come, in one of those rare moments when the parts that had been there for years finally clicked to form a picture, it was a jaw-dropper. That picture quickly got clearer and bigger.

It was a type of predation which is usually unrecognized and almost always unpunishable. It's apart from outright crime and from mental illness. Nor is it just arrogance or simple unpleasantness. It's deliberate, to a degree which may range from barely conscious to carefully calculated. It operates behind various smoke-screens and probably always has. The current you're-not-responsible mentality suits it admirably.

For more than a decade I've observed and analyzed this leeching phenomenon. To say I've come to believe in real vampirism would not be quite accurate. I know it exists. But not with the supernatural creatures of myth. Instead it's behavior we all encounter in ordinary life, sometimes on a daily basis. The blood that's drunk is not the fluid that runs in our veins, but the psychological equivalent: our mental and emotional energy.

Every time I deal with him I come away wiped out.

I walked out of that meeting feeling like everybody there had taken a bite out of me.

She's been leeching off me forever.

A real bottom feeder.

Pound of flesh.

What do you want me to do, open a vein?

These are figures of speech, and our usage of them is often humorous. Sort of.

But I'm willing to bet that by now, most readers already have a situation in mind, maybe several, where they've been drained emotionally by a particular individual, perhaps on a continuing basis.

The cost may be low-level: coming away exhausted, irritated, foggy-minded, much more so than the interaction itself should demand. Often there's a secondary effect: mentally reliving the encounter over the next hours and days, trying to understand what we did wrong, or to deal with our anger, which continues to cut into time and energy.

And the consequences may become far more serious.

Let's call this *emotional vampirism.*

A DEFINITION

Emotional vampirism results from people who crave more emotional energy than they can engender on their own. Therefore, they drain victims of energy in order to empower themselves.

Whether this process is symbolic or actual is a topic of debate between Kathleen Rhodes and myself. Her introduction (which follows this) takes the former view, examining emotional vampirism in terms of conventional psychology; mine, that the energy exchange is actual, along the lines of the long-recognized phenomenon of psychic vampirism.

Either way, we want to emphasize these points:

- Our intention is to identify behavior, not to label individuals: behavior which is destructive, and which can be overcome.

- Most or all of what we're calling emotional vampirism can be explained in other ways: passive aggressiveness, codependency, borderline psychosis, desire for attention or control, con artistry, manipulation, and/or simple rudeness.

 This model has many limitations, but it also has the advantage of being clear and straightforward. Everybody knows how vampires work.

- Whatever one might think of the concept, the emotional cost to victims of these kinds of interactions is real.

Emotional vampires are even slicker than their legendary counterparts (if not as dramatic), usually working undetected. They come in a wide range of types and employ a wide variety of tactics, sometimes very sophisticated, to keep victims off balance psychologically and drain them emotionally. To at least some degree, they're aware of what they are doing: as a general rule, the more aware they are, the more powerful they become.

The overall damage caused by emotional vampirism is huge, from minor harassment that fatigues and impairs victims' concentration, to serious psychological injury involving careers and personal lives. In extreme cases, it can cause mental imbalance and self-destructiveness.

As all this fell into place, I started looking for evidence to support or discount it. When I noticed behavior that suggested emotional vampirism, I'd focus on it, then try to explain it in conventional ways. Most of the time that worked. But often enough, there was clear predation taking place: someone deliberately draining someone else of energy. The picture continued to grow.

I also took a hard look at vampires in legend and literature, and got another surprise: the bloodsucking fiend of fable sheds some very interesting light on the everyday reality.

THE REAL TEETH IN THE MYTHS

If supernatural vampires in fact exist (not just ghoulish criminals with an affinity for blood), they're even more clever than their fictional counterparts. Despite occasional claims from lurid elements of the press, no classic vampire has been unearthed.

And yet this figure maintains an extraordinarily powerful grip on our imagination. Vampiric beings have been held in terror in most parts of the world from earliest times, and in some places, still are. There's an enormous amount of folklore, much of it recorded as fact. Its origins are complex, but an obvious link lies right beneath our skins.

"For the blood is the life," the Old Testament declares, and certainly there's no more vivid symbol of the life force that drives us than blood. For openers, it's highly visible, and there's a power inherent just in the sight, a shock value, an instant focusing from wherever our minds might be drifting—especially if it's our own.

Associating blood with life itself is a short step. In the world of our ancestors where our legends arose, the slaughter of animals—and humans—was commonplace. Victims diminished and died as their blood spilled out, yielding power to the slayers—who in some instances actually drank the blood. The cause-and-effect equation was a simple one, which most people observed firsthand from infancy.

With the evolution of primitive religions, another factor entered. Humankind began to think in terms of a spirit world. For whatever reasons, the connection between that world and physical harm was an early one. Creatures who thirsted for blood—evil spirits of numerous sorts, and/or the dead—appear in mythologies from all eras and cultures.

One response to this was sacrifice, both animal and human, also well established in our earliest records, and also practiced universally. Appeasing—or feeding—those bloodthirsty entities, in the hopes they'd leave the living unmolested, was one of its chief purposes. In the *Odyssey,* Ulysses sacrifices sheep and barters their blood for information from the dead. The Egyptian sun-god Ra bought off a rampaging leopard with blood. "Gehenna," usually a variation of hell, refers to a valley near Jerusalem where children were sacrificed to Moloch. Aztec priests were still ripping the hearts from living victims when the Spanish arrived. The sacrifice of Christ's blood to save humankind is a keystone of Christianity, and sacrifice in religion continues worldwide today, usually, but not always, in symbolic forms like offerings or penance.

It's not hard to see how the idea developed of creatures who sustain their existence by consuming the life essence of humans.

Vampire passion continues today: innumerable film versions of *Dracula* and spin-offs, with new vampire movies released frequently; the immensely popular novels of Anne Rice and others; *Bunnicula, The Vampire Rabbit* and *Count Duckula* for the kids; a pervasive vampire motif in pop culture; and on and on.

A fascination this powerful begs to be explained, and there have been many approaches. One theory has it that vampire legends are primitive attempts to explain wasting diseases which weren't understood medically. Sensible as far as it goes, this explanation leaves many aspects unaccounted for, including the continued interest in modern times.

Conventional psychology tends to view the supernatural as a sort of black sheep relative who occasionally shows up to embarrass the family. When the subject is discussed at all, it's cautiously, with much care taken to make clear that such beliefs are in themselves primitive and infantile.

However, myths may be acknowledged to point to deeper psychological truths, interpreted in various ways, and one perspective on vampirism is much catchier than the wasting disease theory. Some see it as a symbol for, you guessed it, sex. The vampire is the ultimate seducer, draining away resistance until the victim reaches the supreme climax of death, with blood as the operative metaphor. It's also suggested that the vampire's bite may signify sexual awakening or coming of age.

This is illuminating, though not an entirely satisfactory explanation. Seduction certainly plays a part in emotional vampirism. This is another point we'll return to.

A less scholarly take might also point to a fair amount of plain, no-frills fear, and the perverse pleasure it sometimes brings us (particularly at a distance). Here, the vampire holds a special place. Werewolves, mummies, Frankenstein's monster, flesh-rending aliens lurking in spaceships, resurrected dinosaurs, giant spiders in sewers, and all their ilk are put out of the adult mind with comparative ease. When the movie is ended or the novel closed, we may laugh shakily or exhale in relief, but we adjust quickly to the fact that there really are no such creatures.

But the vampire is not so easily dismissed. He—and it may well be a she—is a deceptive, subtle, and powerful creature. He appears outwardly just like anyone else (at least when he's not in full-blown, fang-gnashing, cape-swirling drag), living unsuspected among humans, and even fiendishly courting the trust of those he plans to destroy. He may assume feral shapes, become invisible, pass through walls, summon storms. His lifespan may last centuries and he is exceedingly difficult to kill.

Most horrifying of all, the vampire's bite turns innocent victims into evil, bloodthirsty creatures like himself. They enter a nightmarish shadow existence, neither alive nor dead, but undead—*nosferatu*—and are themselves forced to destroy others to sustain their existence. It's a fear that goes even beyond death, with more than a hint of demonic possession, of hell itself: of losing our souls, that inmost part of being that makes us what we are.

▼　▼

We (the authors) think that still another reason for the fascination lies in our deep-seated, if often unconscious, awareness of emotional vampirism, and the very real damage it can cause. We'll continue to examine legends, as they apply to specific types and situations of emotional vampirism, throughout the book. For now, let's take a look at two (really opposite sides of the same one) as examples of how they can be interpreted in everyday terms.

First, the classic vampire fears and hates sunlight. (Another vivid image may spring to many minds: the snarling fiend crumbling to mummy dust when Dr. Van Helsing rips the curtains from the windows.)

Silly, by any rational standard. But for *sunlight,* substitute the word *exposure.* Like many predators, emotional vampires operate best by remaining hidden: secrecy may be their single most powerful survival skill. They're at home in a world of psychological haze; euphemism, double-speak, and half-truth are their valuable tools; and they very much dislike clear, no-nonsense scrutiny of problems—especially those they cause.

As we've noted, the burgeoning no-fault mentality suits them admirably.

Second, the other side of the coin: the vampire has the ability to create fog and storms.

One of emotional vampirism's most important tactics is to cloud victims' minds. This may happen in numerous ways, over a long-term interaction, or a short, unexpected assault. If it's successful, this confuses and weakens the victim, allowing the predator to employ further energy-draining techniques: working under cover of the fog he's induced. The victim may even find it a pleasurable sort of mesmerism—at least until, if, he realizes he's been ripped off. In many forms of emotional vampirism—particularly long-term, close relationships—there's a large gray area of victim consent (a complex and difficult topic, which we'll touch on in chapter 7, "Up Close").

But a great deal of emotional vampirism—and what this book is mainly concerned with—is more like an unpunishable type of rape: interactions which are forced on victims, and drain them without their consent.

Vampirism may often be portrayed as sexy, but there's not much romantic about this. They're doing it *to* you, not *with* you.

In the following pages, Kathleen Rhodes looks at emotional vampirism from a conventional psychological perspective.

EMOTIONAL VAMPIRISM IN ANOTHER LIGHT

Kathleen Rhodes

Are vampires more than the stuff of myths, legends, and scary tales told to young children? According to Daniel Rhodes, the answer is yes: there are vampires who are real emotional predators.

In this conceptual framework, an emotional vampire is an individual who creates a form of human interaction that in some way forces a reaction, or the expression of energy from another individual—the victim—which temporarily satisfies the predator's craving. This type of interaction results in a decrease in the mental and psychic energy of the victim. Presumably, this involves more than just creating a state of generalized emotional turmoil and confusion: the energy is directed toward, and absorbed by, the emotional vampire himself or herself, although the precise mechanism for this is a matter of speculation.

The literary notion of vampires conjures up images of ghoulish supernatural creatures who are powerful bloodsucking sexual predators. They drain their victims of life-sustaining blood, exemplifying the penultimate monster who "loves" his victims to death. The selection, seduction, and taking of the victim result in a climactic intermingling of aggressive and sexual instincts, destroying one party and strengthening the other. Once victims are completely drained of life-sustaining blood, they become the "undead" and may be transformed into vampires themselves.

The perspective of emotional vampirism differs from the literary characterization in that emotional and mental energy are sought instead of blood. This energy is symbolic of blood, and is the essential currency of the transaction.

Certain techniques are used by the emotional vampire to achieve this unequal exchange. "Task-blocking" is simply preventing a job from getting done. "Turnaround" may follow task-blocking, with the victim being the one blamed for the failure. Inappropriate gifts and unreturnable favors are ways of binding the victim to the emotional predator in a manner that makes severing the relationship difficult or impossible.

"Vectors" and "stacking" are two other phenomena which generate a similar emotional response, of confusion and anger. Vectors such as pets or automobiles are instruments used to tamper with the victim's emotional tranquility. Stacking is the accumulation of several unrelated incidents that cause a series of petty annoyances. The overall effect on the victim is an accumulation of frustration and anger leading to an overreaction or inappropriate response to an otherwise trivial matter.

This typology of emotional vampirism is based on several characteristics, including the strength of the predator and his degree of premeditation or awareness. The *relatively benign* (RB) vampire is the least cunning and potent, who creates only minor annoyances. Unless stacking is also employed, the impact of these is usually not significant. The *merely troublesome* (MT) is more powerful and clever. The *actually dangerous* (AD) predator resembles his counterpart in literature, a fiend of horrifying power and stealth.

At his worst, the emotional vampire is characterized in this model along those lines: self-centered, cunning, and compulsively seeking the excitement of emotional turmoil. He acts with little regard or empathy for others, thereby establishing an identity for himself at the expense of the victim.

In practice, individuals of this sort are extremely rare, and most emotional vampirism is far less intentionally destructive and far more complex, intertwined with other motives and factors. Victim response, in itself, largely defines emotional vampirism: a notion which will prove helpful when we discuss how to recognize, manage, or combat this destructive interaction.

From Daniel Rhodes's description, we can delineate the essential characteristics of this type of predation:

(1) The interaction is destructive or harmful to the "victim."

(2) The victim is an unwitting and passive participant in the interaction.

(3) The interaction enhances the power or strengthens the predator by a mechanism that is unclear or unknown.

(4) The act that strengthens the predator has a transitory and temporary effect. It therefore must be repeated to satisfy the emotional vampire.

(5) The style of interaction is compulsive in that the predator's behavior is repeated over and over.

There are conventional approaches to understanding such destructive, aggressive human behavior. The origins and interactional nature of such human behaviors have been described in the literature of psychology, psychiatry, and sociology. The concepts of aggression, manipulation, dependence, and codependency are competing traditional explanations. Transactional analysis, psychological game-playing, neuroticism, emotional hunger, and borderline personality disorder provide other perspectives which have been used to explain the interactions which Daniel Rhodes describes as emotional vampirism.

The technique of "task-blocking" can be viewed as a form of passive-aggressive behavior. Psychoanalytic and drive theories might attribute such "vampiric" behavior to a variant expression of the aggressive instinct or drive. The aggressive drive, or death instinct as described by Freud, has a biological basis and operates on a hydraulic model. Destructive urges build and must be discharged to reduce tension. Failing to express the aggressive drive was thought by psychoanalysts to be unhealthy and to lead to illness.

To give a simple example: Mary was presenting a draft of a new policy to be reviewed by the hospital committee. She had asked the secretary, Betty, to distribute copies of the draft policy prior to the committee meeting. Betty agreed, but she also remembered a negative employee evaluation she had received from Mary. Betty conveniently called in sick for three consecutive days before the meeting. Betty could not directly refuse to complete the assignment because she feared the consequences. Being ill, however, she could not be expected to perform this task.

The "turnaround" technique could easily be explained as

manipulative behavior or, in transactional analysis, as game-playing. Turnaround is basically a form of blaming others or using the mental mechanism of projection to protect the ego or self from expressing anxiety, humiliation, or ridicule.

To continue with the example, Mary confronts Betty for her failure to distribute the copies of the policy before the meeting. Betty, somewhat righteously, says she was sick and that Mary should have known she would not have an opportunity to complete her task: thus Mary becomes the one in the wrong, for acting unfairly.

A conventional psychiatric explanation of "stacking" might include the following: as frustrations occur in daily life, tension builds within the person as the effects of unmet needs accumulate. When direct expression of aggression is prohibited, or is considered to be risky, the frustrated person acts in indirect and covert ways to express his aggression.

Inappropriate gift-giving and unreturnable favors may be seen as a form of manipulation. One party wards off anger and rejection by attempting to bind the other party closer through emotional or physical gifts.

Some theories suggest that such behavior is learned through experience. Through direct observation of others and through modeling of one's own behavior on that of others an individual learns aggressive as well as other behaviors. Learning also occurs through vicarious participation, as in movies, television, and books. Soap operas present ample opportunities to observe dramatic and intensely emotional, destructive, and manipulative human interactions.

Psychological explanations for this type of behavior focus primarily on the individual identified as the emotional vampire in Daniel Rhodes's perspective. The conventional concept of codependency and the description of psychological game-playing from the transactional analysis model provide traditional explanations for similar interactions.

Transactional analysis suggests that game-playing is a way of structuring time to satisfy stimulus hunger. Psychosocial game-playing does not produce enjoyment or fun. It is a serious transaction involving ulterior motives with predictable outcomes. The roles of victim, persecutor and rescuer feature prominently in psychological games as described by transactional analysis.

A psychological game has four basic parts. These are the *hook, maneuver, gimmick,* and *payoff.* The game of "Yes But . . ." is frequently played by dieters who say that they want to lose weight. The hook, "I've got a problem with my weight," leads to the maneuver, which elicits suggestions from others regarding low-fat diets, exercise, and other techniques. When alternatives and suggestions are proposed, they are met with the response of, "Yes, but. . . ." The game-player's gimmick is never to accept the suggestions, and to counter them with reasons why they are ineffective. The result is the discounting of the basic value of each idea as it is presented. The payoff comes when all suggestions have been rejected. The attitude conveyed is a put-down, and suggests that the would-be helper is not as smart or knowledgeable about weight loss and weight control as he or she thought.

These games we play may temporarily satisfy stimulus hunger. In the transactional analysis perspective negative strokes are better than no strokes at all. Instead of stimulus hunger, the vampire model describes a need for emotional or mental energy, a psychological hunger.

The emotional vampire-victim interaction seems, in some instances, to qualify as a codependent relationship in conventional psychiatric terms. A codependent is a person who has allowed another's behavior to affect him or her so strongly that the person becomes obsessed with controlling or changing it. The codependent begins as a victim, often as the child or spouse of an alcoholic or a chemically dependent person. The focus then may shift as efforts are made to assume the role of rescuer to help the person stop drinking or using drugs. When the rescue attempts fail, as they ultimately will, the rescuer then becomes the persecutor. In essence, all of the person's efforts and energy have been focused on reacting to the problems and behaviors of the individual needing help. But the codependent does not act; she only reacts. This process parallels the development of emotional vampire behavior as described by Daniel Rhodes.

Stimulus hunger which is satisfied by psychological game-playing is similar to the neurotic's hunger for mental and emotional sustenance. Neurosis, no longer included in modern psychiatric terminology, was once a major focus for psychoanalysts. Always greedy for affection, the neurotic either refuses or deprecates any tender feelings offered. Consequently the person suffering from a neurosis is perpetually hungry, seeking affection, excitement, and drama. If no such stimulus is available, the neurotic person creates it.

The modern psychiatric category of borderline personality disorder comes to mind when neurosis and emotional vampirism are discussed. Vampiric behavior is in many ways analogous to the borderline personality disorder. Persons with this disorder show a pattern of unstable and intense relationships. They experience chronic feelings of emptiness and will go to great lengths to fill this emotional void. Interactions with others are frequently infused with intense and often inappropriate emotions such as anger, anxiety, irritability, and sadness. They fear abandonment by others, either real or imagined, and may frantically attempt to maintain relationships and to create emotional responses in others by suicidal threats, gestures, self-mutilation, and other drastic measures.

Relationships often take on the character of "all or none" with either idealization or devaluation of the other person. All people, including those with the disorder, are viewed as completely good or entirely bad, with no middle ground. Although persons with border-line personality disorder fear rejection and abandonment, much of their behavior creates intolerable emotional turmoil and results in pre-cisely what they seek to avoid—the termination of the relationship.

The concept of emotional vampirism is superficially appealing: a convenient and intriguing explanation for many of us who feel depleted and drained by daily interactions with people who seem self-centered and calculatingly narcissistic.

Destructive forms of human interaction and behavior do occur and have been described since the beginning of written history. Daniel Rhodes's observations about the underlying nature of such destructive interactions offer a fresh and entertaining perspective on some aspects of the conduct seen in business and social situations.

But are vampires real? I disagree on this point. As a metaphor, emotional vampirism provides a vehicle for illuminating some aspects of human behavior. The vampire as symbol may have some validity and utility in understanding certain forms of human inter-action, but the notion of the vampire as a real flesh-and-blood entity operating in the world today lacks credible evidence. To maintain that emotional vampires are among us solely by observing the effects they produce is not sufficient evidence of their existence. Such reasoning is no more valid than saying that "disturbed humors" cause disease, when the only evidence for such humors is that disease exists.

Psychology and psychiatry have traditionally drawn on myths, legends, and symbols to describe and explore various facets of human behavior. Freud's Oedipus complex and his analysis of dream symbols are cases in point. We need to remember, however, that myths, legends, and symbols are cloudy mirrors of the real world at best; they do not have elements that correspond directly with the empirical world we live in. They are stories reflecting good and evil, weakness and strength, and horror and cowardice. They may frighten or inspire, but they remain stories rather than realities.

The model of emotional vampirism has limitations. The boundaries of what constitutes vampirelike behavior are blurred, and there may be an inclination to interpret every petty annoyance and frustration as the malevolent workings of an emotional predator. A drive in commuter traffic or an automobile journey to a shopping mall provides ample opportunity for frustration, but does not usually represent emotional vampirism.

The labeling of a person's behavior as vampiric can lead to unintended consequences. Labels can be powerful devices. They can be used as justification for taking hostile actions against others. Calling a woman a "witch" in Salem in 1692 usually led to persecution, and sometimes death.

The focus of this book, therefore, is not to label individuals as emotional vampires. It is rather to explore, recognize, and understand certain human behaviors, to increase our understanding of ourselves and others, and to learn to regulate our responses in order to move beyond the role of victim.

Daniel Rhodes has captured the imagination by drawing parallels between the literary vampire and the emotional predator. As a metaphoric device, *Vampires* sheds light on the nature of destructive human interaction, and reveals aspects of covert and manipulative behavior. Recognition of these roles is essential to developing mastery over such events. Whether one is "victim" or "predator," one may become aware of one's own behavior and its effects on others, and can learn effective ways of responding to such behavior.

Here are a few points that both authors agree on.

WITCH-HUNT

Between about 1300 and 1700, Europe (along with the well-known instance in this country of Salem) was scourged by literal witch-hunts: the origin of the term that has since been generalized to describe other unjust persecutions. Tens of thousands of people—by some estimates, over a million—almost all women, were put to death as suspected practitioners of magic.

It may seem that a low-level witch-hunt is where we are heading. As Kathleen Rhodes points out, there's danger in labeling. But there's a flip side, too. In general, refusing to recognize problems for fear of giving offense allows them to flourish. It's another way that real victims suffer further, and it's precisely those who are generous and vulnerable that emotional vampires are likely to target.

Earlier, the point was raised that emotional vampirism depends strongly on the confusion of true victims with not-so-true ones. Even a little study of historical witch-hunts makes it clear that the situation was the reverse of how it was presented. The real victims were the alleged witches, and the real evildoers, their persecutors. Parallels exist throughout history, right up into the present. Crimes are fabricated; blamed on an ethnic, religious, or political group; and used as justification for the oppressed: The victims are identified as criminals, and vice versa.

Emotional vampirism as we are describing it is not as grim, but it has this in common: it thrives in unclarity, in situations in which what's really happening is very different from how things might seem on the surface. We will continue to point out examples of this throughout the book.

Whatever hunting is going on, the emotional vampires are doing it: not the other way around.

IT'S NEVER THAT SIMPLE

- In themselves, none of these ideas are new. We may be putting them together in unusual ways.
- Our scope is extremely limited. This is not about people who can't help it—if the behavior is genuinely uncontrollable, then it's not emotional vampirism—and we're avoiding the complex and sensitive issues of actual crime and violence (including abuse and battering), mental illness, and most family interactions. Those are topics for much more cautious, in-depth treatment.
- Both men and women engage in emotional vampirism. (In the text, we'll alternate "he" and "she" randomly.)
- Although much emotional vampire behavior may seem childish, we're not talking about kids. This is oriented toward adults.
- Emotional vampirism is not often clearcut. Most falls into swampy ground, mixed up with other factors and causes. Much of it is situational: the individual will turn vampiric only when hard-pressed psychologically. Emotional vampires may well include our friends and loved ones—and ourselves.

Virtually all of us have tendencies toward emotional vampirism, and yield to them to some degree.

- Where there are demons, there are angels. Emotional vampires are offset by their opposite numbers, who act as sort of human batteries, replenishing others with energy and care: a Mother Teresa, a dedicated teacher, a helpful bus driver. (If we seem amiss for not concentrating on them, we can only say, that's not this book's job. We're trying to point out the cutpurses prowling the aisles while the crowd's watching the show.)

THIS BOOK

In general, the better our understanding of any phenomenon, physical or mental, the better we're able to control it, and/or limit its power over us. There's no way to stop emotional vampirism. But there are ways to deal with it.

First and foremost comes simple recognition. We'll describe characteristics, probable situations, and methods of some common types of emotional vampirism. There is of course a great deal of overlap and variation; as in other aspects of human psychology, rarely do individual cases correspond entirely to a model. Our aim is to give enough basic information for readers to be able to extrapolate.

We'll also suggest means of countering emotional vampirism. These are by no means foolproof, but they'll help some of the time in terms of the outward, material costs to victims, and most of the time, in lessening the inner, emotional drain.

This book is intended as a field manual, to prepare readers for a journey into hostile territory—which, in fact, most are already in:

it provides straightforward and concrete information to help spot emotional vampirism in situations where it's common, and combat its destructive effects.

It is our sincere hope that this will make it harder for emotional vampires, in general, to operate.

1

Identification

There are such beings as vampires; some of us have evidence that they exist. Even had we not the proof of our own unhappy experience, the teachings and the records of the past give proof enough for sane peoples. I admit that at first I was skeptic. Were it not that through long years I have train myself to keep an open mind, I could not have believe until such time as that fact thunder on my ear . . .

The nosferatu *do not die like the bee when he sting once. He is only stronger; and being stronger, have yet more power to work evil . . . he can, within limitations, appear at will when, and where, and in any of the forms that are to him; he can, within his range, direct the elements; the storm, the fog, the thunder . . . he can grow and become small; and he can at times vanish and come unknown . . .*

41

*For, let me tell you, he is known everywhere that men have been.
In old Greece, in old Rome; he flourish in Germany all over, in
France, in India, even in the Chermosese; and in China, so far
from us in all ways, there even is he, and the peoples fear him at
this day. He have follow the wake of the berserker Icelander, the
devil-begotten Hun, the Slav, the Saxon, the Magyar . . .*

*The vampire live on, and cannot die by mere passing of the
time; he can flourish when that he can fatten on the blood of the
living. Even more, we have seen amongst us that his vital faculties
grow strenuous, and seem as though they refresh themselves when his
special pabulum is plenty. But he cannot flourish without this diet.*

*He cannot go where he lists; he who is not of nature has yet to
obey some of nature's laws—why, we know not. He may not enter
anywhere at the first, unless there be some one of the household who
bid him to come; though afterwards he can come as he please. His
power ceases, as does that of all evil things, at the coming of the
day. . . There are things which so afflict him that he has no power,
as the garlic that we know of; and as for things sacred, as this
symbol, my crucifix. . .*

Bram Stoker, *Dracula* (1897)

I n the best film version of *King Solomon's Mines*, Deborah Kerr (as
an Englishwoman in search of her husband, who's lost in
uncharted Africa) and Stewart Granger (her guide, legendary hunter
Alan Quatermain) come to a village that's deserted, although the
cooking fires are still burning: the villagers have hidden at the
strangers' approach.

"But where are all the people?" Ms. Kerr asks, puzzled.

Granger, scanning the surrounding jungle for an ambush,
replies grimly, "*I* can see them."

THE THREE MAJOR TYPES

The following chapters will get more into specifics, including examples. For now, we suggest that emotional vampirism can be divided (something like Caesar's Gaul) into three major types: the *relatively benign* (RB), the *merely troublesome* (MT), and the *actually dangerous* (AD).

These terms correspond roughly to the three environments we will discuss: namely, on the street, at work, and up close. There are exceptions and areas of overlap, with lines blurring according to circumstances.

The cost in energy to victims—as well as material consequences—can also be roughly graded along these lines. The most draining interactions will tend to be long-term, and to involve the most vulnerable emotions.

On the street, where the relatively benign emotional vampires prey, the hit is likely to be a flare-up of anger, intense but short. The energy these predators are seeking can be thought of as roughly akin to self-importance, obtained through low-level aggression.

In the workplace, where the merely troublesome emotional vampires prowl, the anger and frustration may be of a longer, slow-burning variety—and there's a chance of real damage, to life and career. Here, the energy being sought is control obtained through manipulation.

True actually dangerous emotional vampires are rare, but such vampirism in personal relationships may fall near or in that category. These predators want the energy that is closest to the victim's emotional center—and life. It's obtained through conscious destructiveness.

In all cases, there are likely to be spin-off costs. We've men-

tioned a few—guilt, ongoing confusion, reliving the experience—
and we'll note others as we progress.

Baseline Criteria

Our first priority lies in distinguishing true emotional vampire
interactions from the vast array of other causes of negative behavior.

Let's start with a few simple, concrete criteria. No one of these,
in itself, is conclusive. But an important aspect of emotional vampirism is that similar types of behavior tend to be repeated, by the
same individual, and tend to come in patterns. If you notice more
than one of these characteristics, more than once or twice, it's time
for a closer look.

Task-Blocking

An individual works, subtly, to prevent you from accomplishing
one or more tasks, even if the goal is outwardly mutual.

This can be a simple one-shot deal with a stranger. A theme
with infinite variations goes something like this: you need a copy of
a document from a city office; a clerk lowers his newspaper long
enough to insist that you fill out a requisition form and return in
three weeks, when the document is sitting in a filing cabinet a few
feet away.

Far more troublesome are extended interactions, often job-
related, where a co-worker or even a boss makes it impossible for
you to complete a project. The goal may well be one you're supposedly working on together. You're sure you're doing your share of the
work, and in desperation, you may even start doing your partner's—

and yet, no real progress is made. Typically, it's difficult to assign clear areas of responsibility, and if you try to do so, it just adds to the confusion.

If you express your concern, the other person will probably be quick to agree. But if you look closer, you may sense that he's not really disturbed. And as soon as you turn your attention away, you'll be stalemated again.

The situation will probably start driving you crazy long before you consciously realize what's going on.

Turnaround

This is probably the single most widespread and effective weapon in the arsenal of emotional vampirism. It's likely to follow assaults of all kinds, and with some—like task-blocking—it's as classic as a right cross after a left jab.

An individual injures you, psychologically, emotionally, or even materially—and then tries to turn it around so that you are to blame. A classic example happened recently to a friend of ours. An acquaintance of hers at work borrowed two chairs and failed to return them. When our friend began to ask, politely, when she might get them back, the acquaintance responded angrily—and then reported her to the police for harassment. The chairs themselves paled into unimportance compared to her anger and frustration.

If turnaround succeeds, it's a vampiric coup: a double-whammy. You have not only been drained by the initial encounter(s), you then get conned into accepting that it's your fault, with attendant confusion and guilt.

Turnaround is often oblique, with blame being shifted to the victim indirectly, rather than openly. It can take several forms: a general lashing out, in which you're included (a bicyclist careens through a red light and narrowly misses crashing into your vehicle, then shouts at you that drivers are assholes who won't share the road); the stance that if you don't like it, it's your problem (a neighbor maintains a steadily growing rubbish pile or other nuisance; when you complain, he tells you to build a fence); and so on. Another variation seems increasingly popular these days: someone behaves unacceptably, you object, and he informs you that *you* have an attitude.

Turnaround would seem to be easy to spot, but this is a place where the emotional vampire's ability to create fog figures in significantly. Its success rate is surprisingly high, and almost always at least plants doubt in the victim's mind.

Diversions

Particularly in long-term interactions, the emotional vampire will often throw petty stumbling blocks in the victim's path, to distract, frustrate, and irritate. The result is constant, low-level exasperation, often at a barely conscious level.

These obstacles won't be directly related to the assault: their main intent is to divert your attention away from it, although they will definitely add to the loss of psychological energy. They are most likely to be ways of punching subliminal buttons you may not even know you have.

But the emotional vampire knows where they are and how to push them. If you suspect you're dealing with one, look closer at petty, random annoyances that keep cropping up—a small item that gets borrowed continually and not returned, or one that is carelessly replaced; minor eyesores in an otherwise neat environment;

the presence of noise when you are trying to concentrate; frequent last-minute interruptions to scheduled plans—and see if they form a pattern.

In general, emotional vampires are acutely sensitive to the mental states of others. They have an acute awareness—an echo of the classic vampire's ability to see in the dark. If there is a window of time when your guard is down and you are especially vulnerable, even a few seconds, that is when an assault is most likely.

If the emotional vampire senses a victim catching on, he will go to extra lengths to throw out a smokescreen: distractions; a sob story; an unexpected concession, as in a task-blocking situation.

Inappropriate Gifts and Unreturnable Favors

An individual presses gifts on you that you don't want to, or can't, reciprocate, and which are difficult to refuse. Often these will come without warning, unrelated to holidays, birthdays, etc. They may be things that are useless to you—but expensive. This will be especially true if he has plenty of money and you don't.

Here, we are not talking ordinary gift-giving, helping out, or the sorts of favors common in business relationships. The key words are the qualifiers: *inappropriate* and *unreturnable*. The object is not to express affection or appreciation: it's to put the victim in debt.

Unreturnable favors are a parallel variation, and may involve things like sex, career advancement, even just affection and company.

This can get a notch more sinister: the individual inflicts the injury, psychological or emotional—and then gives a gift. This probably won't be obvious or straightforward, like a young man bringing his girlfriend flowers to make up for a fight. No direct apology will be mentioned, and usually there'll be a time lag. The victim will probably not put cause and effect together, but the emotional vampire is sending a subconscious message: he is buying his right to bleed, and ultimately, to own, the victim. If he's successful, the relationship may last for years, with potentially devastating consequences. The victim may become little more than a life-support system, and after he has been sucked dry, he's likely to be discarded for fresh provender.

This level of operation may indicate a highly conscious, actually dangerous, emotional vampire at work.

The following criteria depend more on intuition, but may be valuable particularly in situations where there are no hard edges.

These are most applicable to short-term interactions, although they can be good early warning signs for longer ones: for instance, to help you recognize an emotional vampire with whom you're going to have to work.

Come Here Often?

This is a good test for separating emotional vampirism from garden-variety rudeness. After you've been hit by a suspected vampire, and the interaction has stewed around in your mind a while, ask yourself if you sense that the individual is very familiar with the scenario: that this is something he does frequently.

Let's look at a low-level example: you ask a polite question from a secretary or plumber (or doctor, lawyer, or almost anyone else), and you get nailed by an immediate, hostile response. While you are standing in shock, trying to understand what you did wrong, perhaps he gets off another shot, an unpleasant comment, or insult;

rejects whatever apology or defense you might sputter; and/or practices turnaround: it is you who annoyed him.

As the incident replays in your mind, your anger will probably include annoyance at yourself for being caught so flat-footed. But stop and think about how far ahead of you he was, at every step of the way: as if it was a practiced routine. You might even start to suspect that the encounter was not nearly as spontaneous as it first seemed.

Learning to recognize emotional vampires is really playing catch-up ball. In public, an emotional predator may have his eye on you, and even start moving toward you, before you've seen him. In closer situations, the emotional vampire may start setting up ways to ensnare you before you realize he exists.

Give some thought, too, to what the individual was doing at the time. Emotional vampires are adept at appearing busy—but a closer look will often reveal that their outward activity is in fact aimless. First glimpses can be very telling. We'll return to this idea.

Walking Wounded

Most adults who rub shoulders with the world are not overly thin-skinned. Did your anger, degree of upset, time spent reliving the incident, seem out of proportion to what happened? Are you still thinking about the encounter hours, or days—or years—later?

Did it short-circuit your satisfaction in whatever you were doing? Make you decide to cancel a planned activity, because you no longer felt up to it? Do you get the sense that you were pushing a giant rock uphill, and absorbing hostility, for trying to get someone to do what was really, after all, only his job? Did you sense that he—perhaps beneath a blustery façade—was fundamentally undisturbed, or even enjoying himself?

The Vampiric Signature

Finally, let's add a most curious phenomenon, the vampiric signature.

This is a good one to pay attention to. It's a mysterious thing: a warning sign the emotional vampire may project—not unlike certain dangerous flora and fauna in nature—unintentionally or even unwillingly.

Not always, but often, emotional vampires will say or do something to let you know you've been had. This may clearly contradict whatever façade they have been using: almost as if they are going out of their way to identify themselves. It will often happen after the encounter, or not be noticed by you until the emotional vampire is gone. Or, as mentioned above, it may occur during your very first glimpse of the predator, long before you have realized what is going on.

In street-type hits, the signature is likely to be a gesture that is contemptuous in some roundabout way. (Examples are given in the next chapter, "A Day in Heck.") With more personal encounters, it will probably be something that causes you exasperation: an object you're fond of, which the emotional vampire has handled and gotten dirty or damaged slightly, or some sort of mess he has made and left you to clean up. A visitor, particularly one who may be inconvenient or unwanted, may leave something behind, ostensibly forgotten, which you have to go to some trouble to return. (And we're *not* talking about a lady leaving an earring at the apartment of a man she'd like to see again.)

As with inappropriate gifts, there's an element of mocking genuine practices of respect and affection. And once again, that mind-clouding comes into play. The vampiric signature is almost always noticed, but rarely recognized for what it is.

2

A Day in Heck

Here sighs, with lamentations and loud moans,
Resounded through the air pierced by no star,
That e'en I wept at entering. Various tongues
Horrible languages, outcries of woe,
Accents of anger, voices deep and hoarse,
With hands together smote that swell'd the sounds
Made up a tumult, that for ever whirls
Round through that air with solid darkness stain'd,
Like to the sand that in the whirlwind flies.
I then with horror yet encompassed, cried:
"Oh master! what is this I hear? what race
Are these, who seem so overcome with woe?"

Dante, *The Inferno* (c. 1321)

We are all aware of the various tangible economies the world operates on: food, products, trade, and such, with the overall medium of money. There are other, less visible economies, such as energy. Specific to this book's concerns is the mental and emotional energy exchanged in the ebb and flow of human interactions.

Personal energy can be thought of as a type of money, and its daily expenditure as an allowance, or budget. We start each day with a set amount, which is ours to use. At the end, the account will be depleted—we're mentally and physically fatigued. But, assuming good health and no misfortunes, we have the reasonable expectation that the next day it will be replenished.

We can spend our energy on activities, give it away to others, get an immediate payback, invest it in hopes of a long-term return . . . or get ripped off.

Let's look at a day: not exactly typical, but a fair sampling of activities that many people are likely to engage in. This is a rough sketch. Readers are invited to color in their own situations and experiences. It will be helpful to keep in mind the criteria listed in the previous chapter.

We'll also introduce two oblique (okay, sneaky) emotional vampire techniques: *vectors* and *stacking*. In brief:

- Vectors are external, secondary means, usually physical objects, which emotional vampires use to make assaults. These are not weapons in the usual sense. Vehicles, pets, and sports paraphernalia are a few favorites.

- Stacking involves a series of emotional vampire predations, usually minor and unrelated, which in themselves may go almost unnoticed, until one pushes you over the edge and you blow up. Usually at the wrong person.

And don't forget the vampiric signature.

THE HITS

It's a Friday in June. You live in a suburb of a good-sized city and work downtown. You have a couple of business projects in development, with an important meeting scheduled for the afternoon. This evening, you plan to make dinner for someone you have become romantically involved with fairly recently.

You are in the habit of enjoying, or at least punishing yourself constructively with, an early jog in a nearby park. It's a pretty morning, the day's business looks exciting, and at the end, there's the payoff of seeing your lover.

You're enjoying these thoughts, planning details, and dreaming a little as your body settles into its exercise rhythm. . . .

Then WHAM! Out of nowhere, there's a dog streaking toward you, low to the ground, barking and snarling. It lunges for your ankles and nearly draws blood. You stop, yell at it, stamp your feet. The dog circles, still snarling, trying to get at you.

Then you realize that a young man is approaching. He's also yelling, not at his pet but at you. He may actually be threatening: *If you touch that dog, I'll*—(Physical assault is not unheard of, although most emotional vampires will shy away from it.)

You stare in disbelief. By now your whole system is pumped full of adrenaline and your blood pressure is heading through the ionosphere.

The owner kneels to soothe his pet, glaring at you, and continues to berate you. His dog would never hurt a flea. It only *seemed* to be trying to bite you, and only because *you* scared *it*. And so on. His language and tone are angry, even abusive.

You manage to calm down enough to reply. The dog attacked while you were minding your own business; the owner is violating courtesy, good sense, and possibly the law, by walking the animal unleashed.

He counters readily and smoothly: it's a terrific bummer dealing with people who hate dogs. This angers you all over again: that has nothing to do with it.

You may realize—although probably not until afterward—that his anger is quickly gone. Instead, he shifts the exchange into a pointless, but now mild, argument. The confrontation may go on for some time (probably, as long as you let it).

The encounter ends without apology or admission of wrongdoing. Man and pet (which has long since wandered off to sniff in the bushes; its job done) move on. You may get the sudden odd sense that they are not really going anywhere, even for a walk. That they came out of nowhere, as if they had been hanging around waiting for someone, like you, and now both are off to find someone else.

You may finish your run, or give it up early. Either way, your tranquility is shattered. In fact, you probably won't be able to think about much of anything else for a while.

Your drive into the city includes a stretch of two-lane road, curvy and narrow, with a 45-mph limit. Most of the traffic consists of people like you, trying to get somewhere safely. You are a careful driver, in the habit of frequently checking your mirror. You glance once and all is well behind.

When you look again thirty seconds later, there's a vehicle *right there*: a few feet behind your bumper. You're so startled you jerk the wheel.

The vehicle maintains the close distance, edging impatiently in and out of the lane as if to pass. You check your speedometer, in case you have been dawdling, but you are going just over the limit. The road is tricky, and your attention is strained, dangerously distracted by the antics behind.

You reach a straight stretch, clear of oncoming traffic. You slow and move as far as you can to the right, inviting the vehicle to pass.

But now the driver, in clear exasperation, has dropped back fifty yards. You're relieved, thinking he's accepted the reality of the situation; it's only another mile until stoplights begin anyway.

But when you look a few seconds later, he's coming fast again, and he stays on your tail through the final, winding stretch.

In town, the road opens into a four-lane strip, lined with stores, fast-food places, and gas stations. You expect that the driver will race by you, in his haste to get wherever is so pressing. Instead, he hangs back, in no hurry now. Next time you look, he's turning leisurely off into a convenience store or coffee shop.

Your company's board of directors meeting is coming up, and producing the annual report has been your responsibility. Last week you sent it to the printer; this morning you call to make sure everything is progressing smoothly.

A secretary asks you to repeat your request, then puts you on hold. It's clear that this is already a nuisance to her. After some time, you get cut off. You dial again. She tells you impatiently that she's still checking. You spend more time on hold. Eventually she returns and tells you that they never received the package.

You feel the stirrings of panic—the deadline is approaching—and ask her if she's absolutely certain. Her voice sharpens a notch as she assures you she is. You will have to send them another copy.

Luckily, you have copies of the proofs, although you have to scramble to make sure everything is there and in the right order. This takes a chunk of time you had planned on spending on other important business, and you remain worried that you have forgotten or misorganized something.

There's no time left to mail it again. You decide to drop it by the printer's yourself on your way home.

▼ ▼

The day's main event is a meeting about a marketing project you have been trying to develop. The idea was yours to begin with, and you know it's a good one. At some point along the way, a senior colleague expressed interest, and offered to work with you on it. This would be mutually beneficial: your creativity and energy, teamed with his experience and influence.

Or at least that was how it seemed. But that was several months ago, and not much has happened. You have continued to work on the idea, to feed him the material you came up with, and to gently push the process along.

But he doesn't seem to have done much from his end. Your work stops in his office. He discusses ideas as if he is about to act on them, but they remain potential, then fade, replaced by new ones where the same thing happens. He frequently cancels meetings, which destroys the momentum you have tried to build. His main attention usually seems to be on other work, and he may have let you know—perhaps sharply—that your project is relatively small compared to others he has to manage.

But at other times, you are pleasantly surprised—and confused—by a burst of enthusiasm, or a step ahead he has taken on his own, or an unrelated favor (such as tickets to a play or game you probably have no interest in seeing), all of which has kept you hoping.

Still, the project remains deadlocked, and the situation has really started to drive you crazy. You find yourself worrying about it at odd times (like the middle of the night), which is affecting your performance on other fronts. You may even have decided that in spite of his clout, you would be better off on your own, yet he's involved so deeply by now that you cannot untangle the project or yourself from him, and you don't dare go over his head.

But it looks like all will end well. Your colleague has (reluctantly) agreed that today's general staff meeting is the time to make your pitch. This is particularly important to you because he is about to leave on vacation, followed by vacation season in general: it will be impossible to get any kind of consensus again for months.

Out of deference to his seniority, you agree that he should do the talking in the meeting. He assures you that he is turning his attention to this, and he will have taken care of things from his end.

But in the meeting, when he starts the presentation, it quickly becomes clear to you that he has done nothing. He repeats ideas you have given him—using *we,* as if their development had been mutual—but they don't come together in any conclusive form. It's obvious that no one is impressed, and equally obvious that he realizes this.

He closes with the statement that the project would be farther along if he and his co-workers had been able to agree on certain fundamental issues. Although he doesn't name you, it is clear to everyone that you are who he means. The implication is equally clear that you, as the junior partner, have been unwilling or unable to grasp the wisdom he has tried to impart, and that is what has stymied the project.

You leave the meeting stunned. He stops you in the hallway. You note how hale and fit he looks: glossy, good-humored, ready for a few weeks of golf and sailing. There's no mention of what just happened. Instead, he wonders if he could ask you a small favor. Since you live not far from him, would you mind stopping by his house to feed his goldfish while he's gone?

You still have to stop by the printer's with the replacement manuscript. The drive is forty-five minutes out of your way, through nightmarish rush-hour traffic, but you make it just before they close. There is absolutely no place to park for blocks. You spot a small deli with half a dozen spaces. In desperation, you pull in. You hurry inside and explain to the counterman that you will only be a minute, and offer to pay him. He's young, and seems indifferent; he waves away your money and assures you it's no problem.

The secretary in the printer's office is on the phone, with what sounds like a personal call. She continues to talk, without acknowledging you, until you finally interrupt her. With one hand over the mouthpiece, she tells you impatiently that they found the package: it was delayed in the mailroom. There's no trace of apology, either for the mistake or for her failure to call you and save you the trip. She waits coolly, eyebrows raised, as if asking if you are finished bothering her.

As you turn to go, your gaze catches a manuscript on her desk. You realize it's the original of your carefully prepared report, rescued from the mailroom. It strikes you as odd (again, probably not until later) that it's on display here; this is a reception office, with nothing else that suggests copyediting or proofreading.

But you notice then and there the highly visible coffee cup stain on the title page.

Back outside, the first thing you see is a large older man, wearing an apron—not the counterman you spoke to, but perhaps the deli's owner—stuffing a sheet of paper under your windshield wiper. Even from half a block away, he looks angry. You hurry to explain, but he doesn't see you until he's stepping back inside.

When he spots you, he says something you can't hear and gestures threateningly at the CUSTOMERS ONLY sign, then turns his back and goes in.

The note is a crude scrawl: ASSHOLES GET TOWED.

You make your way home, perhaps aware that you're on edge: more sensitive than usual to the jostle around you, impatient at small delays. As you drive that same stretch of two-lane road, a vehicle comes to a stop at a crossroad, a few hundred yards ahead. There is plenty of time for it to pull out, and you slow a little in case it does, but it just sits there.

Then, when you're within fifty yards—speeding up again, confident that it can't possibly make the turn now—it does, edging slowly forward into your lane. You start to slam on your brakes, but the oncoming lane is clear, so you swing out and pass. As you go by, you lean on your horn and shout angrily.

It's then that you see the white hair and hunched shoulders of the elderly driver. When you look again in your mirror, you realize that she's terrified. Guilt and shame crash-land on you. Normally polite and mild-mannered, you have turned into a screaming demon, causing real risk to both her safety and your own.

You may start to understand that your energy bank balance is hovering near the red. You have been getting more and more frustrated all day, and you are finally wiped out: exhausted mentally and physically, scattered, unable to concentrate, and angry. Whoever is normally in charge in your mind has been crowded out by these emotions. The result is that you flounder, performing tasks mechanically, drifting in a fog, and not a very pleasant one. Your normal well-being depends on that vitality that has gone missing. It's connected with your innermost sense of *self*.

You finally get home, maybe have a drink or a bath, and start to settle down. It's been a rough day, but it's over, and a recharge, in the form of a pleasant dinner with your lover, is on its way.

Time passes. He's a little late, and then later. After an hour, you call to make sure everything is all right. There's no answer; you reach his machine and leave a message.

The evening grinds slowly on, with no show and no phone call.

Along with annoyance, hurt, and worry, you recall small faults in him that you have overlooked. You are a neat housekeeper, but you have noticed that he has a habit of handling objects thoughtlessly as he wanders around, leaving a small chaos behind. This exasperates you, even though you feel silly about it, and chide yourself for being compulsive.

Finally you go to bed, but in spite of your exhaustion you can't sleep: you're hurt, disappointed, confused—and the tapes of everything else that happened during the day buzz around in your head like flies. Some time after midnight the phone wakes you from a restless drowse. It's your lover. At first you are miffed, but he assures you that you told him the date was for *tomorrow* night. You are quite certain he is wrong, but when you say so, *he* starts to get miffed, and you back off.

You agree to reschedule for tomorrow, and you tell yourself it was an innocent mistake. But besides the spoiled evening, more uncertainty starts to gnaw. Is it accidental that he made no effort to explain where he was until this hour? You can't help wondering if he was alone when he called.

And you remember that something like this happened once before, when you first started seeing each other: at the last minute he canceled a date you had carefully planned. Some time after, for no apparent reason—although likely at a point when you were confused, down, wondering if he cared for you at all—he brought you a surprise gift: a bottle of perfume (or necktie, if "he" is a "she"). It wasn't something you would have chosen for yourself, or are likely to use. The thought even crosses your mind that he had bought it for someone else, then never gifted it, for whatever reason. Still, it was a pleasant surprise. He was at the peak of his charm and considerateness, there was especially good sex, and your doubts were put to rest.

Which, with variations in detail, is just what happens this time.

THE TALLY

There is an old joke about the scoreboard at the Roman Colosseum: Lions XXXVII, Christians 0.

Let's total it all up.

You absorbed two hits from public predators before your day even began. Both used vectors: a dog and a motor vehicle, respectively.

The dog owner's assault seemed practiced. There was a strong feeling that he had been through this before, perhaps often—even that he was out looking for it. He did his best to shift the interaction into a silly argument. After his initial hit, he made the telling move of turnaround. The fault was yours: you frightened his pet, out of your dislike for the species.

The cost to you: besides the initial shock, you probably feared a dog bite or the confrontation turning violent. (In fact, neither was likely, but while the predator knew that, you did not.) You came away feeling bad, angry, confused, and at least slightly guilty. *Did* you do something to frighten a harmless animal? Unbeknownst to you, do you carry a hostility to canines that they can sense?

These types of encounters are almost guaranteed to flare up in your mind repeatedly. While you try to work them through, you relive your negative emotions all over again.

This is an expensive little chunk out of your emotional energy bank.

In the second case, you can be reasonably sure you encountered a road warrior emotional vampire, and not just a childish driver (although there's a lot of overlap). Telling details include the particular techniques he used—the zooming rear approach out of nowhere, the impatient antics, the failure to pass when he had the chance. And the vampiric signature can be detected when he turned leisurely off in town, making sure you knew he was in no real hurry.

Yet another moderate-sized chunk of your emotional reserves is gone, before you've even made it to the office.

We will classify both of these encounters as relatively benign. This is not entirely satisfactory, because, particularly in the second instance, there was physical danger involved. But we're talking in terms of the psychological component. Physical harm is almost never an emotional vampire's intent.

(It can, however, be a troublesome possibility, as can the flip side: victims with low boiling points may react physically to emotional vampire assaults, particularly public ones; such as, by taking a swing, or, like our victim when driving home, being goaded into dangerous behavior. Besides the injury this can cause in itself, it can bring tangible social sanctions, like law enforcement, into the picture. Should this happen, the trouble, possible expense, and resulting hammer hanging over the victim's head, will tend to make him much more docile in the future, which emotional vampires are quick to sense and take advantage of.)

The situation with your colleague at work is far more serious: a definite merely troublesome interaction. (It is not actually dangerous, because there's no strong emotional tie, but it's close. The relationship is personal as well as professional, and he is in a position to damage your livelihood.)

Here we see classic task-blocking, over a long period of time, with occasional diversions to keep you off balance. There have also been small gifts and favors in the form of influence: his way of buying his right to continue. This is followed by a particularly vicious turnaround, in which you are taken to task in front of your employers.

Finally, there comes the telltale signature: after he hits you hard, he asks you to do him a favor, while he goes on vacation.

The cost to you, not just emotionally, but in hard, practical (and long-range) terms is huge.

Many relatively benign encounters (e.g., the secretary at the printer's or the deli owner) are hard to separate from garden-variety thoughtlessness or rudeness. With the secretary, the task-blocking was low-level, and could have been a mistake. But there was also an implied turnaround: if the situation was not exactly your fault, you were certainly a nuisance. Perhaps more telling, she was very much on her own turf, and way ahead of you every step of the way. As with the dog owner, this had the feel of something she had done before, a game she has developed over time.

You may also find yourself going out of your way to make excuses for her. She has a lousy job. She is sick of doing menial work for people who obviously make more money at more interesting positions. Your manner or tone offended her.

In fact, you were only asking her to do her job, and not a very difficult one. Such attempts on your part to rationalize someone else's behavior can in themselves be telling: they mark you as having the mind-set of a likely victim. And don't forget that coffee stain on top of your report.

Besides the substantial time and trouble that it cost you, it also led to the parking encounter (and was one more bale in the stack that was building). This situation may have been an honest mistake, or the counterman's negligence. It's a little hard to believe that in a small business he is not aware of his boss's strong feelings about something like parking.

Or you may have run into a team: in this case, something like a good cop/bad cop routine, except the object was not to get information, but to hit on a victim. (Teams come in many variations, and can be quite serious. We will discuss a few.)

Of all the incidents, this one in itself is the least significant. But it was precisely what it took to bring your exasperation to a head about all the others, and keep you steaming on the way home.

Which was what led to the next: your blow-up at the elderly driver. You got stacked. All the previous hits added up, until, without realizing it, you had reached critical mass.

As usual, besides the immediate energy loss, there are spin-offs. In this case, your guilt for your unfair reaction will make you easier prey for subsequent attacks.

As noted, stacking also makes any overreaction on the victim's part particularly vulnerable to outside sanctions, like social disapproval or law enforcement. Your friends (or the police) might sympathize with you about the dog assault. But if you run an elderly lady off the road, no one is going to be impressed by your tale of a bad day.

Last, but far from least, comes the miscommunication with your lover. This seems innocuous, and it may well be. But you also may be dealing with a serious merely troublesome, or even an actually dangerous situation.

Much emotional vampirism, including most of the above incidents, are in the realm of exasperations, and may even contain an element of humor. But there is nothing funny about interactions where you are on especially vulnerable emotional turf.

There are several warning signs. A pattern has started to appear: an emotional upset inflicted on you, which has an air of calculation (especially in allowing the suspicion to linger that he might have been with someone else); turnaround, in blaming the miscommunication on you; diversions, in the form of subliminal annoyances around your house; and inappropriate gifts, as oblique rewards. It all has a smooth, even practiced, feel.

These are the hardest predations to perceive, and to break.

Finally, it's worth noting that in all of these cases, the emotional vampire was careful to operate in a manner that did not risk any kind of sanction. All the behavior was outwardly random and/or unintentional. And you had no chance to defend yourself.

Mercifully, most days are nowhere near like this one.

Once again, we are oversimplifying: these examples are both exaggerated and unusually clearcut. But if you are out mixing it up with the world, the odds are high that encounters roughly similar to any one of them—although isolated rather than strung together —will occur with some regularity.

We will close this chapter with a suggestion, now that we have given some concrete examples of emotional vampirism in action. If you have an experience along those lines (or remember one), and want to examine it in this light:

- Recreate it mentally (the sooner, the better).

- Be as objective as you can: note exactly where you and the other person were, and what you were doing, when you first became aware of him; *why* you became aware of him; who spoke first, and said what; and give as accurate an account as you can recall of the words and gestures of the exchange. Writing it down will very likely help.

- Reexamine it. File it, in your mind or your desk. If it is long-term, keep a running account; if short-term, accumulate any similar ones that occur.

Situations will come clearer, patterns may emerge, and—perhaps most important—you may start seeing future ones in time to head them off.

3

Combat

It is the most unexciting contest you can imagine. It takes place in an impalpable grayness, with nothing underfoot, with nothing around, without spectators, without clamour, without glory, without the great desire of victory, without the great fear of defeat, in a sickly atmosphere of tepid skepticism, without much belief in your own right, and still less in that of your adversary. If such is the form of ultimate wisdom, then life is a greater riddle than some of us think it to be.
Joseph Conrad, *Heart of Darkness* (1899)

In the modern world, the day-to-day struggle most of us engage in is more likely to be mental than physical, and the blood we shed, energy. In a similar vein, psychological methods of combating vampirism must replace the gory ones of old.

69

A few preliminary points:

• A reasonable, straightforward counter to any emotional assault may be all that's required: simply asking the other person to stop the bothersome behavior.

But if you're dealing with a true predator, this is not likely to solve the problem. It may even be another way the emotional vampire manages to escalate the cost. In short-term interactions, they tend to be adept at ways of prolonging the contact and energy drain: feigned misunderstanding, pointless arguing, even a show of anger (as with the dog owner in the previous chapter, "A Day in Heck").

In longer interactions, and/or with merely troublesomes, direct confrontation may even backfire more seriously. For instance, in the workplace, the emotional vampire—particularly if he's better established than you—may be in position to undermine your job. Let's face it, you're not likely to come out on top if you accuse your boss, or a senior colleague, of being a vampire. In such situations, more subtle forms of self-defense may be advisable.

One exception can be useful in some circumstances, particularly street-type hits, where you're not concerned with long-term consequences: turning around turnaround, by the simple expedient of saying, when you recognize the tactic beginning, "Don't try to turn this around on me."

This is essentially a form of sunlight—letting the emotional vampire know that you recognize what's happening—and can blunt an attack, or even stop it cold.

• If possible, in any sort of assault, withdraw. Particularly in street-type predations, there's nothing for you (but plenty for the emotional vampire) to gain by sticking around to argue. Think of yourself as a sandwich, and the emotional vampire as the teeth.

• Particularly in relationships, such as with "A Day in Heck" 's troublesome co-worker, you may be able to withdraw step by step, in a sort of running dogfight: taking each hit as it comes, recognizing it for what it is, and defending yourself as well as possible, using other techniques. In the long run, the emotional vampire is likely to look for easier prey. Glimmers of sunlight may help: subtly letting him know that you sense something amiss beneath the surface, but stopping short of outright confrontation.

• Humor can be an effective first line of defense. (If you're good-natured enough to muster it. Many people aren't.) Simply grinning and continuing on your way can serve like protective armor, and may in itself deflate the assault. Or you might try a more edged response, such as telling the secretary from "A Day in Heck" that you admire her: you wish you had the courage to dress so inexpensively for work.

But it's not always effective or even appropriate. Particularly in serious matters, laughing things off won't make them right, or make the situation go away.

• In any event, keep your temper. Losing control will almost always play into the emotional vampire's hands (recall, again, our dog owner). Your emotional intensity will be greater, providing richer fare. The interaction will almost certainly be extended, providing more of it. And your loss of clarity will make it easier for the emotional vampire to convince you that the fault is in fact yours. Not to mention the possibility of your ending up in jail, and/or getting sued, if the confrontation gets violent.

• Stacking—when your anger builds from several unrelated events —is particularly hard to recognize. The single best way to deal with it is to be aware of your fraying nerves. Individual assaults will still take their chunks, but you're not likely to blow up at that last straw—like "A Day in Heck" 's little old lady driver—if you see it coming.

• No defense is going to work one hundred percent. Many kinds of short-term hits simply can't be stopped. About all you can do is cut your losses. If you understand what's happening and why, they will be easier to handle, and you will have a better chance of seeing them coming.

• Finally, it's one thing to sit in a room and think all of this over, but quite another to deal directly with a difficult situation.

Defending against emotional vampires will be frustrating and discouraging at first. On the face of it, they are holding all the cards, and in any given situation, they will be several jumps ahead. While victims are going unsuspectingly about the business of living their lives constructively, emotional vampires are watching for a chance to nail them. But as with anything else, improvement comes with practice. And in most cases, you can minimize pain, guilt, and energy loss.

In the following pages, Kathleen Rhodes offers some conventional techniques, learned firsthand through many years of clinical experience, for defense against emotional predations.

▼ ▼

SUGGESTIONS TOWARD EMOTIONAL PREDATION MANAGEMENT

Kathleen Rhodes

Any conceptualization of emotional vampires as malevolent and consciously evil results inevitably in a portrayal of interaction as conflict, and of combat as the appropriate response. The traditional and accepted psychiatric models of human behavior stress a different approach.

Clinicians prefer to use the terms "intervention" or "management" rather than "combat" when describing their responses to clients and others. Combat refers to a fight, battle, or clash between parties or armies, as in war. We combat disease, but we intervene with patients and clients to help rid them of the disease or to stop its progression. If we cannot eliminate the disease, we focus on developing management strategies to ameliorate the effects of the illness.

The clinician-client relationship provides a framework and establishes certain rules of conduct for both the therapist and the client. It is not a friendship relationship in which there is give-and-take with mutual satisfaction of needs. In a professional relationship the needs and interests of the client are foremost. The overriding obligation of the clinician is to provide the best help or therapy for the person seeking his/her services. The management strategies presented here are derived from the conventional psychiatric conceptualization of roles and professional relationships.

Emotional vampirism is not an accepted clinical concept, but I will use Daniel Rhodes's terminology for the sake of simplicity and clarity. As we noted earlier, emotional vampirism occurs within the context of an interaction between at least two parties, the emotional predator and the unwitting victim. The engagement of the victim by the predator has a primary goal of eliciting an emotional response. By creating this expression of emotional or mental energy, the emotional vampire is able to satisfy his craving or hunger. He is no longer empty and has made his mark by temporarily establishing his identity.

Let us be clear: the interventions discussed here focus on the process of *not being a victim.* We are not trying to change the behavior of the emotional vampire. To avoid victimization, we need to understand ourselves, and to recognize the nature of the interaction.

Understanding ourselves is an ongoing process in which we discover strengths, weaknesses, habits, and predilections in our relationships over time in a variety of experiences. It is never-ending and continues as long as we live.

There are particular features of character or personality that make one vulnerable in these interactions. Are you vulnerable? What do you know of yourself that would make you easy prey for emotional vampirism? As you look at yourself, ask these questions:

(1) Do I need to be in command or control of situations and/or people?
(2) Do I need to be seen as a very nurturing or caring person?
(3) Do I need to be recognized, complimented, and flattered by others frequently? Do I need to be "liked" by others?

Do I need to be in command?

The need to dominate or take control manifests itself in a variety of ways. The underlying dynamic is the need to define a situation for others. This may take the form of being an authority on a given subject, and being the strongest, smartest, or most expert, the absolute best at a given pursuit. The driver who slows down to force a speeding driver to comply with posted speed limits may be a typical and commonplace example of one who needs to control the behavior of others.

A psychotherapist who prides himself on treating patients with drug abuse problems and personality disorder attempts to engage a patient in therapy. The patient refuses any contact or conversation with the therapist. The therapist suggests that physically forcing the patient to come to his office would make therapy possible. We can imagine the emotional and physical turmoil this action could engender in the patient if undertaken. Whether this illustrates emotional vampirism, and on whose part, is debatable, but it does show that the need to dominate others can be a powerful lure or attraction.

The need to dominate can clearly lead to power struggles. One can recognize when one has been a participant in a power struggle by examining the interaction and the feelings experienced as a result of it. The key ingredient is that one participant attempts to exert power over, control, or overpower the other.

In many power struggles no one wins completely, and both parties retire from the conflict feeling emotionally drained and in turmoil. In others, there is a clear victory for one participant, and the loser suffers alone. Such struggles result in intense emotions of frustration and anger.

For an emotional predator, the emotional storm created by a power struggle can be quite satisfying. Once an emotional predator identifies individuals with a need to control others, those individuals can be set up to repeat the power-struggle pattern over and over. This is a form of the psychological game of "Let's you and him fight."

Elizabeth related a pattern of interaction in her family that illustrates how power struggles can be precipitated by a third party.

When Elizabeth was a teenager, she was rebellious and quick-tempered. Her father was domineering, and exacting in his demands for respect and obedience.

Her mother seemed passive, and unable to assert herself with either the father or the daughter. When Elizabeth disobeyed her she would say, "Just wait until your father comes home!"

In one instance, Elizabeth was an hour late returning home from a group activity at church. When she arrived home her father yelled at her from his bedroom through the closed door, telling her she was irresponsible and lazy. He told her that her mother worked hard, and that Elizabeth did not do her chores around the house.

Elizabeth could hear her mother whispering to her father, but could not hear what she was saying. The father continued to yell at her, telling her that she was grounded until he told her otherwise.

Elizabeth was angry and exasperated. She had worked very hard cleaning the house, and had completed her chores. The accusation was incorrect, and doubly angering because it was unjust. She yelled back at her father, "One day I will go where I want when I want, and you won't be able to stop me!"

Again she heard her mother whispering, but could not tell what was said. A moment later her father bounded out of his room, grabbed Elizabeth, and began beating her with his belt. Through the doorway Elizabeth saw her mother, a smug, self-satisfied smile on her face.

Elizabeth strongly believes that her mother set up many arguments between her father and herself. She saw this pattern repeated over and over.

After one has been in several power struggles, one can begin to identify the opening maneuvers. Individuals can often recognize the pattern of the interaction and can foresee what will happen. In my own experience I often get a slight churning in the pit of my stomach, signaling me that emotional conflict is present, and that it is time to detach my emotions from the encounter, and reassess what is happening.

One of Aesop's fables has helped me rethink my behavior when I am tempted to engage in a power struggle. The blustery North Wind and the Sun are debating as to which is the stronger. They look down to Earth and see a man walking alone, wearing a coat. They agree that the one who could get the coat off of the man will be considered the stronger.

The North Wind blows fiercely, but cannot blow the coat off. The man only clutches his coat closer and tighter to his body. The North Wind blows and blows, but its frigid efforts fail to remove the coat.

The Sun smiles, and takes its turn. It glows, and shows brilliantly. It spreads its light and warmth . . . and the man takes off his coat.

The lesson for me is that I cannot force, command, or coerce another person to change his behavior. I can only create circumstances and conditions which facilitate the person's choice to change.

Do I have excessive needs to nurture or care for others?

All humans have a need to nurture and care for ourselves and others, but the need can become excessive and compulsive. The need to nurture can become so great that it dictates a large part of our interaction with others. This has jokingly been referred to as the "Nurses's disease."

The need to nurture makes a potential victim attractive to the would-be emotional predator. There are two important aspects of the nurturer that make her particularly vulnerable. First, the excessively nurturing person's sense of self or self-image is largely dependent on the role of nurturer. Second, the nurturer frequently finds herself in codependent relationships which involve emotional turmoil. (Codependency is a relationship between at least two parties in which one party, the would-be rescuer and nurturer, is so involved with the life and problems of the other that he or she actually facilitates the other's dysfunctional behavior.)

The need to nurture takes the form of excessive kindness and gentleness, often with frequent unsolicited and inappropriate questioning of the health or well-being of the other. The excessive nurturer often makes excuses and fails to have realistic expectations for the other participant.

A busy nurse, intent on insuring that her patient has sufficient food and that the dietary intake is properly recorded on the patient's medical record, may ask how much food was eaten and fail to notice that the patient is tearful and emotionally upset.

Asking questions regarding food intake is consistent with the nurse's self-image as competent and caring. Overlooking the patient's obvious emotional distress, however, is not. In focusing on the amount of food eaten and ignoring the patient's emotional distress the nurse provides an excellent opening for a would-be emotional vampire to attack her as insensitive and uncaring.

Even if one does not see oneself as overly committed to nurturing, one probably likes to be viewed as competent in certain roles. An assault on that competence, especially without merit, can create emotional turbulence, frustration, and anger within.

While we were writing this book, a friend who is an emergency room doctor came to us with the following:

"Let me run one of my ER cases by you. Tell me if this was an emotional vampire attack, or if it has another explanation."

I was working the night shift at the ER. At about 5:30 A.M. I took care of a 45-year-old woman with asthma. She had had asthma for ten years, and was taking the standard inhaler medications with good control. She came to the ER because she was having increasing problems over the last week, ever since moving back into her sister's house (where she would be staying for the next three months). She said her sister had pets to which she was allergic, and that each time she went into the house she had an asthma attack, which was not controlled by her medications.

When I saw her she was not having a severe asthma attack. She was not having any asthma at all: no trouble breathing, no wheezes in her lungs, and no trouble talking. Indeed, she spoke two or three long sentences with each breath, which is not possible for asthmatics who are having an attack. She had an appointment with her asthma specialist in four days. She had a primary doctor through her HMO insurance whom she could have seen for care. She could have waited until 9:00 A.M. and called either of her doctors for a same-day appointment based on the fact that she was having a lot of problems.

Instead, she came here to the ER early in the morning to see a doctor who had no past knowledge of her particular history and needs.

I talked with her and took a history. I examined her, and then proposed that she see her asthma specialist later the same day. She appeared upset and angry. When I asked her about this, she said that I was "nonchalant" about her care and her problem.

We talked some more, and I realized that she wanted me to simply give her a prescription for three-months' worth of Prednisone, a cortisone medication which suppresses the asthma response. She was unhappy with me because I did not automatically and casually give her what she wanted, even though I had reasonably and competently assessed her problem and offered options that were appropriate to her medical needs.

Eventually I gave her one dose of Prednisone, and asked her to call her asthma specialist later the same day to explore other ways of handling her problem, and to let him decide if she should be on cortisone for a longer period.

Afterward I realized that her characterization of my response as "nonchalant" was a blow to my perception of myself as a careful, competent, and caring emergency physician. I also realized that it was absolutely wrong.

This patient came to the emergency room even though she did not have an emergency. She was not in danger of dying from asthma, or even having a severe attack.

She had clearly identified the source of her problem: she had an asthma attack each time she walked into her sister's house. If I had been truly "nonchalant," I would have listened to her for one minute and then said, "Stop going to your sister's house. You get an asthma attack when you go there, so don't go there!"

Instead of casually giving advice, I carefully took a history of her present asthma problem, and of her past history of asthma problems. I asked about her asthma medications, past and present. I asked about other medical conditions she might have, and I asked about other medications she was taking. I asked about allergies to medications. I asked about smoking and other factors that might aggravate her asthma, and I asked about other symptoms, such as fever and cough, that might indicate an infection or other cause for her increasing problems. I examined her lungs and heart. Only after this fairly thorough examination did I discuss with her my findings and possible treatment options. This was NOT a "nonchalant," hasty, or casual encounter . . . and this was at 5:30 in the morning, when she had come to the ER for her convenience, *and not because of any medical need, emergency, or urgency.*

I realized later that her desire for Prednisone was like a person who is hitting his head against a wall and has a headache, and who asks a doctor for pain pills so he can continue hitting his head against the wall without suffering as much pain.

Prednisone is a powerful medication. It is not one that can be prescribed casually. Like all medications, if it is powerful enough to have a beneficial effect, it is also powerful enough to have undesirable or dangerous effects. Prednisone can cause ulcers, rot the bones (hips and spine in particular), and suppress the body's ability to respond to stress and illness. She wanted me to prescribe a three-months' supply; Prednisone is rarely used for longer than a few days or a week or two. When it is used for longer periods, its use needs to be considered carefully, and monitored closely. It is not a medication to be prescribed casually for a three-month period by an emergency room doctor.

Her comment about my "nonchalant" attitude bypassed all my professionalism and reached right into my emotions. I was outraged and depressed, although I did not realize it until later. It took me several hours of thought and analysis to figure out what had happened, and to decide that this patient was wrong.

Certainly her frustration with her increasing asthma problems had become an emotional upset for me. Was this an example of vampirism? Was this "turnaround"? Or was it something else? It certainly made me feel I had failed as a physician . . . until I thought about it for a while.

In this situation, there are objective and subjective signs of covert messages and a hidden agenda from the patient. Objectively, the request for Prednisone was inappropriate in terms of time, place, and person. The patient had a primary doctor and an allergist. Instead of seeking care from these doctors, who knew her and her problems well, she directed her request at a physician who was essentially a stranger, unfamiliar with her particular situation.

She sought care at 5:30 in the morning instead of calling her doctors three hours later; she went to the emergency room, even though she was not suffering from an emergency or even an urgent condition; she asked for long-term care for a recurring condition. In subjective terms, the use of the term "nonchalant" was pejorative and judgmental, in that it implied a lack of careful clinical scrutiny of her problem. It also indicated that she was unhappy because she did not get what she wanted, although she never stated this directly.

The emotional aftermath experienced by the doctor is the defining characteristic of this destructive interaction. His repetitive review of the incident, his questioning of himself and his professional self-image, and the attempt at understanding what had transpired are indicators of an emotional vampire attack.

Recognizing that we have an emotional investment in being thought of as an excellent mother, driver, doctor, friend, or whatever role is dear is the first step in knowing our own vulnerable areas. Once we acknowledge this vulnerability, we can recognize our susceptibility to the opening gambits of emotional predators, which are aimed at taking advantage.

The second aspect of excessive nurturers that makes them prone to establish vampiric relationships is the inclination toward codependency. Codependents often care so deeply for others that they become absorbed in the lives of others and neglect their own needs.

The codependent person is often the spouse or significant family member of a chemically or alcohol-dependent person. Key characteristics of the codependent role are reacting, controlling, enabling, rescuing, and eventually persecuting. Codependents rarely act or respond to issues in their own life, but react strongly to the behavior of the other. They control by taking responsibility for the actions of others, thereby sending a covert message that others are irresponsible and incompetent in running their own lives. They shield and protect others from suffering the consequences of their actions. In essence, they prevent others from learning from their mistakes and enable troublesome behavior to continue. The rescue is not acknowledged or appreciated.

The mother of an alcoholic friend repeatedly rescued her son during his bouts of drinking. The son and his wife lived next door to the mother. When the son began drinking, the wife would become angry and he would move in with his mother for a few days. According to the mother, he was helping her with some major cleaning or remodeling project. The mother provided him with money when his wife cut off his access to funds. Although the payment from the mother was seemingly for the son's work on the project, in actuality it permitted the son to continue his alcoholic binge. Once he had some money he left his mother's house and partied with his friends. When his money ran out, he came back to his mother or to his wife's home. Both mother and wife were ready with pitchforks, and both assumed the role of persecutor, charging him with familial and financial irresponsibility.

Who is the victim and who is the emotional vampire in this example? The participants traded roles as rescuer, victim, and persecutor, with each participant assuming one role or other as the emotional drama unfolded. If the emotional predator is analogous to the persecutor, then each person in this scenario became a vampire at one time or another.

Codependency is an emotional quagmire requiring expert help. If you recognize this pattern in your life, there are therapeutic and self-help programs designed specifically for these problems.

The need for flattery and compliments

The need to be flattered, complimented, and liked is universal in human nature. All humans want recognition and acknowledgment for who we are and what we have accomplished. In psychoanalytic terms, this is referred to as narcissism or having narcissistic leanings. Narcissistic tendencies, however, can easily be read by would-be emotional predators and tend to make one susceptible to an engagement. The greater one's need for flattery and being liked, the greater the likelihood of an encounter with an emotional vampire.

Once these narcissistic tendencies are recognized, the emotional predator can use compliments and flattery to ingratiate and insinuate himself, to bind the other ever more closely, and to involve the victim in an intimate relationship. If the process is successful, the emotional vampire may assume a dominant role in all aspects of the victim's life. Other colleagues and friendships may be demeaned and limited, through being portrayed as unworthy of the victim. The victim spends more and more time with the emotional predator, and less time with others. By degrees the victim is isolated from others and becomes even more vulnerable to manipulation by the emotional vampire, on whom he increasingly depends for satisfaction of his emotional needs.

A nurse who was hired into a management position for the first time described her experience.

When I started as the head nurse of the unit, I had little experience or knowledge of management principles. My co-worker Jeff had worked on the unit for ten years and seemed to know the ins and outs of day-to-day operations quite well. He always managed to speak with me when I was on the unit, and he invariably complimented me on my hairstyle or dress.

I admit that I take pride in my appearance, and like to dress in bright, stylish clothes. Jeff was the only staff member who acknowledged my appearance and seemed to appreciate my efforts to dress well. He frequently consulted me regarding problems that emerged, and seemed to appreciate my opinions and input.

As time went by Jeff began to discuss problems with the performance of other staff members. Eventually, through discussions with Jeff, significant shortcomings in knowledge, skills, or work habits had been identified for virtually all the other staff. As I attempted to tackle these problems, the other staff members were reluctant to speak with me about problems on the unit, or about anything else. Jeff told me that the unit staff were ungrateful and ignorant clods, and that I, with my experience, education, and background deserved more respect that I was getting. Soon my only real communication and information about what was occurring on the unit came from Jeff.

In one situation Jeff related to me that one nurse had been particularly rude to the family of a patient. The family members had questioned why the patient had been given the wrong medication. According to Jeff, the nurse had responded loudly, "We will take care of that. It is no concern of yours!" When I attempted to discuss the situation with the nurse involved, she went to her union representative. She said I was persecuting her and creating a hostile work environment. She organized the rest of the staff to petition my supervisor, stating that I was unsupportive of them and ineffective as a manager. She maintained that what she actually had said to a hard-of-hearing family member was, "We made an error. I'll look into it. Don't worry. We will take care of the problem and we will take care of your husband."

As a result, I was given the choice of resigning or being fired. I resigned. I later realized that the ever-helpful Jeff had set me up.

As the example above illustrates, emotional vampires can use the tools of flattery and compliments to engage and use our narcissistic leanings, resulting in devastating emotional turmoil. Knowing that we desire affirmation of our worth from others and that we crave positive feedback or outright flattery can help us be on guard, and to be wary of compliments given by others.

Evaluating flattery and compliments involves two parts: authenticity and appropriateness. Authenticity refers to the genuineness and creditability of the statement itself. Is the comment a realistic appraisal of a specific accomplishment? Or is it a global, obsequious statement pandering to our weaknesses and needs?

An authentic compliment recognizes definite achievements, is limited to a particular instance, and promotes constructive development. Flattery is phony when it does not reflect what is real, when it extends beyond the current situation, and when it has ulterior and covert aims.

A psychotherapist was pleased with the progress he was making with a very difficult hospitalized patient. The patient was suspicious and for a long period had avoided any interaction with him. He was delighted that he had broken through the impasse in that the patient had made him a cup of coffee and offered it to him one morning.

She continued to offer him coffee each morning for a week, waiting for him to taste the coffee, and then departing. He recapitulated the therapeutic maneuvers he had undertaken and he was pleased by the compliments he received on his success.

At the end of the week a nurse noted that the patient went to the bathroom, came out with a container of urine, and went to the kitchen. The nurse followed, and observed the patient using the urine to make the psychiatrist's coffee.

Compliments and flattery are frequently accepted without question because they feed our needs and appear to be a recognition by another person of the obvious truth of our own worth and quality. Because we tend to accept compliments and flattery uncritically, they provide an excellent opening for emotional vampires.

Whether the example above represents emotional vampirism is unclear. It does, however, show our human vulnerability to special favors, compliments, and gifts, and a need to carefully evaluate special favors and compliments as to their appropriateness and authenticity.

Most compliments are genuine, and are not designed to lure someone into a destructive interaction. Appropriate compliments can be constructive, self-confirming, and stimulating to personal and professional growth and development.

We need to examine and question the appropriateness of compliments before accepting them wholeheartedly. The appropriateness of compliments refers to the timing and circumstances, and to the roles of the people involved. A husband's statement to his wife of "You look lovely in that dress today!" may be very appropriate. If he made the same comment to his female subordinate, it would be inappropriate to their roles, and could be interpreted as sexual harassment.

Identifying whether a complimentary statement is an opening gambit for an emotional vampire can be difficult. Ask yourself the following questions:

- Does it match my own perception of my accomplishments?

- Is it appropriate to time, place, and roles of the involved parties?

If you answer no to the above questions, you may want to ask yourself if there are ulterior motives for the compliments, or if they form a transactional pattern typical of the complimentor's past destructive relationships.

If they are inappropriate, a mere nod of the head without saying anything might serve to discourage future attempts.

▼ ▼

Recognizing one's own susceptibilities and needs is the first step in avoiding victimization. In the never-ending process of understanding ourselves we learn to go beyond the superficial level of "opening maneuvers" to develop insight into the actions of others and into their motives. Once we recognize what is happening, we can move on and correct our perceptions of the interaction to correspond more closely to reality.

Reframing an interaction, or redefining a relationship can take two basic forms, *detachment* or *reengagement.*

Detachment involves removing oneself physically or emotionally and maintaining an emotionally neutral stance. Detachment does not necessarily mean abandonment or not caring for another. It is similar to the professional ideal of being empathetic.

Nurses and doctors are taught to be empathetic rather than sympathetic. In empathy, there is an initial identification of what the other person is experiencing, with a subsequent reobjectification of what is occurring. Identification allows one to more fully understand the other person's predicament. Reobjectification is a process of establishing boundaries, and focusing the problem or issue where it belongs. The empathetic person appreciates the emotional situation of the other, but maintains enough emotional distance that he can function appropriately to remedy the problem and care for the other.

By contrast, sympathy is an identification with another's situation without reobjectification. It engenders feelings of pity and condolence, and does not move toward an objective appraisal of the situation. It is an emotional involvement which may be so great that it interferes with the ability to act appropriately.

A man standing outside of a hospital was pounding on the wall of the building with both fists. A hospital employee walked up and yelled, "Stop!

Don't do that!" The man turned, with fists still clenched, and moved toward the employee.

The hospital security team arrived and they restrained the man. He then began to sob, and told them that his two-year-old son had just died in the emergency room.

The hospital employee's immediate reaction to this man's apparent violence was to have the action stopped. If he had recognized the emotional upheaval present he might have responded in an empathetic manner by observing, "You seem upset by something. What is happening?" The subsequent physical and emotional turmoil of the confrontation with security personnel and the physical restraint of the man might have been avoided.

Opportunities to practice empathy and to develop emotional neutrality occur daily. Instead of reacting angrily to drivers who move too slowly or too fast, consider what else might be going on in their lives. Imagine that the slow driver might be an elderly woman desperately trying to maintain independence and do her own grocery shopping or visit her doctor. The speeding driver might be ill or trying to get to a sick child in an emergency room.

When one realizes that multiple explanations exist for most human behavior, practicing the art of being nonjudgmental and forgiving is easier. It can be good for one's emotional health, and it limits the emotional vampire's opportunities to strike.

In some relationships it is difficult or impossible to detach oneself and assume a position of emotional neutrality. When a parent is near death from incurable cancer, the children may request that the parent receive heroic treatment in an intensive care unit, with intravenous fluids, medicines, and respirators. They may be unable to accept the fact that such treatment will not cure, and will only prolong their dying parent's painful and unpleasant existence. Their emotional response is sympathetic, rather than empathetic like that of the doctors and nurses who are caring for the dying person.

Take also the example of a psychotherapist working with a patient diagnosed with depression, borderline personality disorder, and substance abuse. The patient has made three suicide attempts, two of them seriously life-threatening. Since inpatient hospital stays are limited, the therapist is working toward discharging the patient. Fearing abandonment, the patient begins threatening to kill herself if discharged.

The therapist is faced with a quandary. He must discharge the patient, but he knows that with her history of suicidal attempts, her impulsiveness, and the diagnoses she carries that she may well go forward with her threats of suicide. He feels responsible for the patient and for her actions.

Is he responsible? Should he feel responsible? If she kills herself will he believe that he is the cause? Can anyone prevent the suicide of another? Is the therapist being held as an emotional hostage to his sympathetic feelings toward his patient?

Perhaps the therapist can temporarily forestall the act of suicide. Within the empathy-sympathy context, however, he needs to establish boundaries that mark the point at which his responsibility ends and the patient's begins. While she is in the hospital he can set limits on her behavior, but he cannot control her behavior indefinitely.

The therapist needs to reframe his interaction with this patient by clearly indicating what he can and cannot do. He can gently confront her with her fears of abandonment and her reaction to the possibility, and point out that this is not a real fear, that support and continuing therapy will be provided. He can clearly state that he hopes she will not harm herself, and he can let her know that he sees her as being in control of her own actions.

The therapist can reframe his interaction with the patient in empathetic and supportive terms, important both for his sake and hers.

Another approach to handling emotionally destructive or draining interactions is humor. Humor can be an intriguing device to interrupt emotional upset and foil the would-be emotional vampire.

Healthy humor has the effect of lightening emotional burdens and helping to place an event or topic in a realistic context. It is not designed to diminish anyone or to make anyone the butt of a joke.

Four friends decided to take a long driving trip together. After the first thousand miles they realized that conversations which began innocuously soon became complaints. The grievances covered all aspects of life, including the price of gas, inconsiderate drivers, the foolishness and stupidity of elected officials, the evils of bureaucracy, money-gouging bankers, and the many ways in which schemers take advantage of others. The emotional atmosphere in the car was heavy and dark, and without realizing it, the passengers were reluctant to converse. The joy of the trip was evaporating.

One of the travelers jokingly referred to the back seat as "the grumble seat." The group laughed, and began a pleasant game of limiting the negative contents of the conversation, and limiting the number of "grumbles" allowed each person each day. Exceeding one's grumble allotment for the day resulted in a penalty, such as buying lunch or coffee for the group.

Soon the travelers were monitoring themselves, and when they spoke a criticism they were immediately aware of it, often adding a ridiculously positive statement to avoid being penalized for grumbling. This occasioned much laughter from the others.

The emotional atmosphere lightened considerably, and the party enjoyed the rest of the trip greatly.

Avoiding becoming the victim of emotional vampirism involves knowing yourself and those aspects of your personality that make you vulnerable. It involves recognizing patterns of human interaction and the opening maneuvers of the emotional predator.

Many strategies may be used to intervene in the vampiric process and short-circuit its progression. Among them are detachment and emotional neutrality, empathetic engagement, reframing of interactions in different terms, and humor.

Daniel Rhodes will close this chapter with a few more speculative suggestions.

It's my own belief—not shared by either my coauthor or my publisher—that an actual energy exchange takes place in emotional vampirism, on a level which our senses don't perceive, and that certain vampire legends point to this.

The following ideas involve that premise. Adventurous-minded readers may want to give them a try, along with more conventional techniques.

(Symbols like the cross are used because of their tradition in legends, rather than any intrinsic religious valence.)

Sunlight

Specific recognition of emotional vampirism at work is the first valuable sense to develop. In itself, it can constitute a powerful defense. This has to do with the fact that pain is an excellent teacher. Anyone who has ever done much building, for instance, knows that after you've bashed your nail-holding fingers enough times, they learn to stay out of the hammer's way. In fact, they can actually seem to sense its approach and act on their own, without your brain being conscious of it. Similarly, experienced mechanics usually sense when a wrench is about to slip and take the skin off their knuckles.

Think of emotional vampirism as the hammer or wrench. Something in you will often start to pull back at contact, even before you realize consciously what you're dealing with. You may come to recognize an odd, nonspecific sort of tingle at these moments, as if something in you is lifting its head to look around uneasily.

Noting specifics of your immediate, instantaneous take on the situation—physical location, gestures, body language, words exchanged—can be of great value in identification. Watch for your own body reacting, unconsciously, to assume defensive postures, even though there's no threat of physical danger: turning aside, or moving hands and arms, as if to block something coming at you.

This type of recognition can be a very unsettling experience, especially if there's eye contact.

You can take the sunlight defense a notch farther, either face-to-face or in your imagination. Try keeping your gaze on the other individual's face, but focus your *attention* on the forehead, or the center of the chest. Literally look through as if penetrating a screen.

Silence, coupled with this focus, can be a powerful tool. If you do speak, slightly oblique remarks—rather than responding directly to the matter at hand—will give things another twist.

These are all signals that you recognize the emotional vampire: you've *made* him, in the sense used by police. In itself, that will put a serious cramp in, or even stop, many emotional vampirism hits.

Garlic, Host, Holy Water

In the legends, these are often used to establish barriers the vampire
can't cross. Particularly in long-term interactions, where you can't
withdraw—as with someone you care about, when emotional vampirism is mixed up with genuine affection and you are willing to
give a certain amount of energy—drawing emotional boundaries
within yourself can be effective: you'll go so far but once you reach
that point, you'll shut off the flow by distancing yourself, or even
showing your own teeth. It's a thin but valuable line to walk.

Tourniquet

One of the most troublesome aspects of emotional vampirism predations is that they may keep appearing in your mind for days,
weeks, even years after they're over. It's important to distinguish
between this and the pondering we all do over difficult emotional
occurrences as we try to resolve them. Here, we are talking about
situations where there's nothing to resolve. You realize you've been
had, plain and simple. But the incidents keep repeating themselves,
and you find yourself flaring up all over again. Over time, as with a
leaky gas tank, the costs add up.

First, try the tourniquet: Locate the target the emotional vampire has tapped in your own emotional network: anger, guilt, fear,
and so on, perhaps in combination. Think of the target as a wound.
Actually picture it: your energy bleeding out through your emotional channel. Apply a tourniquet of concentration. Cut off the
flow.

Cross

Next, the cross.

Imagine yourself holding a crucifix. Or, if you prefer, a baseball bat, axe, or chainsaw. Add a means of disposal: an airplane hatch, or ski jump to nowhere, or something more Gothic (like the reception arranged for Banquo's killers in Polanski's *Macbeth*).

Every time the emotional vampire appears in your mind, whack him through the hatch, instantly and fiercely. He'll come back, probably right away. Do it again and again and again. In time, this will become second nature. And in the long run, it will save you a lot of energy.

Biting Back

We don't recommend more draconian measures, like lopping off heads or driving stakes through the heart, even in imagination. But here's a way you can attempt to reverse an attack.

Think of the emotional vampire as having fangs, which sink into your emotions to suck energy. In your mind, grasp them firmly. Turn them back on the emotional vampire and plant them in his haunches. Or, if you prefer, plant them into another emotional vampire you've encountered.

There's a grim amusement in imagining them biting themselves or each other, trying to suck their own blood. (If this seems mean-spirited, remember: they're after yours!)

Like chasing the vampire through the hatch, this should be repeated until it becomes second nature.

If nothing else, these techniques will help take you out of the loop psychologically, especially in situations where more conventional techniques are not effective.

4

On the Street

Like one that on a lonesome road
Doth walk in fear and dread,
And having once turned round, walks
on, And turns no more his head;
Because he knows, a frightful fiend
Doth close behind him tread.

I turned my head in fear and dread,
And by the holy rood
The bodies had advanced, and now
Before the mast they stood.

Samuel Taylor Coleridge,
The Rime of the Ancient Mariner (completed 1797)

In the next three chapters, we'll describe a number of common prototypes of emotional vampirism. In practice, these are almost never pure: there's a great deal of overlap, and mixing of vampiric tendencies with other forms of emotional interaction, including positive ones.

THE PUBLIC BE DAMNED

This chapter will deal with predatory behavior which takes place mainly in public locations, and in which there's no personal relationship with the victims. We'll call this, generically, *public vampirism.*

Public predations are most likely to involve the first, and least powerful, type: relatively benigns. Once again, we're not talking crime or physical violence. Serious trouble may occur in rare instances if things get out of hand, but it's not the emotional vampire's objective.

The type of energy that's desired by this level of predator is roughly parallel to power in the form of self-importance. Rather than acquiring it in genuine, constructive ways, these emotional vampires resort to aggressive "me-first" behavior, low-level bullying, setting up clashes in which they come out the winners, and the like. The initial wound to the victim will usually consist of a brief—although, perhaps, intense—flare-up of anger, compounded by confusion, guilt, etc., and extended by further reliving of the incident.

As with most of the other behavior we'll discuss, less arcane causes can be assigned: rage, desire for petty power, simple rudeness. Probably these figure in most of the time, and may be adequate explanations in themselves. There's also considerable overlap with scofflawing, with attendant justification (i.e., only chumps pay attention to the rules or laws in question).

We'll say it once more: however you choose to look at it, the energy drain on the victims is real.

DOWN BY THE RIVERSIDE

Daniel Rhodes notes:

One odd and interesting bit of legend is that the vampire can't cross running water.

There are a number of explanations for this. Water was often likened to spiritual energy, and flowing water tended to be especially pure. This was hateful to evil spirits, as were certain other substances for similar reasons: iron, believed to come from heaven; salt, a preservative, enemy to the corruption of evil; and garlic, considered to have medicinal properties (sickness and death were often attributed to malevolent spirits), and as a bulb, suggesting resurrection.

But here's another possible bit of explanation that may contribute.

Public emotional vampires tend to be territorial (an echo of another myth, that the vampire must sleep on a bed of his native soil). They'll work a particular area, for as long as the traffic will bear. And the richest feeding grounds will be where potential victims must congregate.

In the old days, there weren't so many of those places. Bridges and river fords were prominent (along with crossroads, other spots vampires were thought to frequent). There might only be one for many miles, with several roads joining, and every traveler having to pass there.

These were prime locations for early emotional vampires to hang out, waiting for prey. Thus this legend evolved, I'm suggesting, not because vampires couldn't cross the water: they didn't want to. They weren't trying to get anywhere. Our ancestors spotted the lurking figures, and made the association.

Like other legends, this eventually got garbled, with religion and superstition, into the supernatural.

In the Introduction, I mentioned the picture of emotional vampirism that built slowly in my mind, and finally clicked into focus. The above evolved out of one of the first parts in that process. For many years, I've been in the habit of running—or more accurately, plodding—a couple of miles in the afternoons, when weather and time allowed. My usual path was an abandoned railroad track. Most of the way was wide open, through an old rail yard and then fields. The people I encountered in those areas were almost always moving purposefully, on their way somewhere.

But there were a couple of narrow creek bridges, and one intersection with a lousy pedestrian pathway. At these, I'd see people who tended to be more stationary: often, the same individuals at the same spots—they'd move from one to another, as if on a circuit— and I'd see them both as I was going out and coming back, meaning they'd been there for some time. Outwardly, they'd usually be busy in an innocuous way, walking a dog, strolling, pausing for a smoke —not panhandling, or harassing, or anything else aggressive. The obvious take was that they were passing by, or just hanging out.

But over the years, the realization started sinking in: if I had some sort of unsettling clash with a stranger—and I'm not a troublemaker, honest; when I'm running, it takes all the energy I can muster to get both feet off the ground at the same time—or if I witnessed one, it was almost always at one of those narrow spots.

I started paying closer attention, watching from a distance, as I approached. Again and again, I'd see variations of similar events: a lone bicyclist who had been fooling around for several minutes, suddenly losing control and colliding with a pedestrian; or a dog owner throwing a stick for his pet, moving gradually closer to an approaching jogger, and finally landing a toss in the jogger's path. Petty stuff—no robbery or violence—but each time, resulting in an emotional clash, and a chunk out of somebody's day.

Strangest yet, while the faces would change over time, the figures would look similar from a distance: moving slowly around the same small areas, as if they were held there by invisible tethers.

Whether or not there's anything to all that, rest assured that there will be a high concentration of public emotional vampires in locations where many people have to pass through—and whatever activity they might appear to be engaged in, the same truth holds as in the old days. The real business is feeding.

Public emotional vampires, and relatively benigns in general, are particularly proficient in the use of vectors. We'll take a special look at vehicle predation, which has skyrocketed over the past years into a low-level, but peculiarly dangerous, problem today.

The sections that follow in italics are from contributors, describing emotional vampire encounters of the types we're discussing.

SPOILERS

At the lowest end of the spectrum comes public emotional vampirism specializing in annoyance. This is often at a distance, in keeping with its weak status on the vampiric scale: it provides a poor energy return, but it's safe. Generically, this type of emotional vampirism literally robs life of its pleasure. Which is more or less its job.

Variations on the spoiler include impersonal phenomena we probably don't ordinarily think of as vampiric. Many of us are so inured to the sight of graffiti marring beautiful buildings in cities, we don't even notice it consciously. If we did, we would probably use the word "depressing": a small energy drain, all around, all the time.

Most outdoors lovers have probably had the experience of hiking somewhere remote, expecting it to be pristine, and finding it deliberately trashed: another thing which leaves, and we think this is a good way to put it, a stain in one's mind.

Unnecessary noise, often created by vectors (car horns and alarms, unattended dogs, slamming doors) may usually be random. But here's one place where a criterion we mentioned in chapter 1, "Identification," becomes particularly useful: if you start looking closer, you may find the same individuals at work, again and again, over a period of time.

In these situations, if you're dealing with a true emotional vampire, asking him to stop is not likely to help. The behavior may pause, but it will return, often in modified form. You've given the emotional vampire an energy hit, by letting him know it's getting to you.

I, like my neighbors in our tightly packed residential neighborhood in Brooklyn, was sleeping peaceably early one Monday morning, all of us, I'm sure, trying desperately for what rest we could get before another work week began. At 4:30 I was slammed awake as rudely as if I'd had ice water thrown on me: a car alarm, not twelve feet from my garden floor window, was wailing, ricocheting off the brownstone canyons, and rattling around in my bedroom. I rolled over, thinking it would stop. Minutes passed. I tried to shut it out, imagining the owner hustling into bathrobe or jeans and jostling outside to turn it off. Any minute now.

Fifteen minutes later, the alarm is still going. There is no phrase to describe my growing fury: fed up? Ready to kill would be more like it.

Finally, after another five minutes of scenarios in my head, I got up and pulled out a piece of paper. I wrote, "It's now 5 A.M., and thanks to you, the whole street is now awake. If you're not here to tend the car, don't use the alarm." I stuck two pieces of tape on it, and for good measure, took an egg out of my refrigerator. I hustled out into the street and taped the note to the driver's side window and then smashed the egg on the windshield. Ironically, the impact of the egg must have joggled the alarm mechanism, because it shut off. I smiled and went back to bed.

When I got home from work, the car was still there, with lovely dried goo dripping into the front. And other people had added comments to my note! It was like a hate petition to the driver.

A friend spoke emotionally about the poverty of her family in the mountains of West Virginia. She recalled one event clearly.

A large box of hand-me-down clothing had been sent by a distant relative who was much better off financially. She knew that there was a daughter in that family, slightly older, and she hoped there would be a dress or blouse for her in the box.

When she opened it, she found several dresses and blouses in her size. She was thrilled, until she looked more closely.

All the buttons had been removed.

TURF EMOTIONAL VAMPIRISM

One prevalent form of public predation involves what we'll call *turf emotional vampirism*: individuals staking out a territory and working it until circumstances make it advisable to move on to another. Once potential victims step on it, they're fair game.

As we've noted, physically narrow spots—the equivalent of bridges—are favorites. Crowded public areas—transportation depots, busy spots in cities, shopping malls, beaches, or parks—will usually attract many emotional vampires, of varying types.

(As a general rule, the more powerful the emotional vampire, the more desirable a locale he will stake out—for instance, an office—and try to maintain it for himself alone. This is in keeping with natural selection, with the strongest hunters claiming the choicest grounds, and defending them against rivals. Larger, busier areas are something like the Serengeti: there's greater tolerance because of the sheer size and amount of provender.)

One popular low-level form of turf emotional vampirism involves taking up premium space (such as lingering at a busy public machine, a telephone, or washer/dryer in a laundromat, that others are waiting impatiently to use).

Physical blocking is a notch up the scale, and may lead to the next step of actual verbal confrontation. A variation on the bridge theme involves staking out a narrow passage (an aisle, building entrance, etc.) where victims are forced to squeeze by, perhaps with jostling and annoyed words. The use of a vehicle to unnecessarily block a street or intersection is a vector form of this.

Aggressive panhandling may combine several of these elements, including blocking, with insults and even threats if you don't pay up.

A more refined variation—the sharp-eyed may pick up on this

—is for the turf emotional vampire to spot a victim some distance away, and arrange an encounter. This has the advantage of seeming accidental, and greatly facilitates the emotional vampire's ability to employ turnaround.

Attacks may also involve a sudden display of irritating behavior: not outwardly aimed at the victim, but so physically close that he's forced to respond. It can take many forms: jostling, gestures, a sudden shout, bursting into song, etc.

Vectors are frequent in this: dogs are a favorite, as per "A Day in Heck." Variations include simply allowing the pup to pester, or—a slicker refinement—maneuvering the victim between owner and pet. Only then will the owner start loudly disciplining it, which will take the form of shouting into the victim's ear or face.

Bicycles as vectors have surged in popularity in recent years, particularly in cities with large youthful populations, like college towns. Roller blades are gaining fast, with the advantage that they can be used in highly urban areas: Manhattan's avenues, for instance. Skateboards are another strong comer. Other types of sports equipment can serve a similar purpose (older boys throwing a baseball near where your child is playing).

A variety of other vectors and techniques exist, most of which non-emotional vampires would never dream of, until they realize they've been victim to them.

Many turf emotional vampires work out of stores, offices, restaurants, etc., where the stream of victims comes to them. (See "Come Here Often?" in chapter 1, "Identification.")

Frequent tactics in these arenas include delays and apparent mistakes being passed off as unavoidable, and/or someone else's fault. Impatience or condescension (the victim is to blame for expecting reasonable service, and/or wasting the emotional vampire's precious time) are common secondary additions. These have the dual advantage of providing cover for the predation, and being yet another oblique form of turnaround.

Traveling emotional vampires might seem to be an exception to the territory rule, but in fact, they have simply learned another adaptation. Their turf is right beside you: typically, a seat in a public situation, as on a bus, train, or plane. The hit may involve obnoxious behavior that you can't escape, or it could be more refined.

I was on a train in England, going from London to a smaller place about an hour away. It was a late afternoon in March, dark, cold, rainy. The train car—an open one, not compartments—had only a few passengers.

A young woman got on. She wasn't much over twenty, quite pretty, and well-dressed. But something about her face struck me as odd. She had a tight, unhappy smile, and restless eyes. There was something childish about it. The word fretful comes to mind. It didn't seem to go with her sophisticated look, and it marred her prettiness.

There were probably thirty empty seats, but she sat next to another young woman, about her age, who was reading. This woman was not as pretty, or as well-dressed. She looked like what the Brits would call a shop girl.

It was another thing that struck me as odd. I'd been in England long enough by then not to expect someone who looked upper-class to go out of their way being friendly with anyone who wasn't.

The first, well-dressed woman started a conversation with the second one, who seemed happy and very pleasant. She put down her book and chatted. I stopped paying attention. They were several seats away, and the bits of conversation I could hear didn't mean anything to me.

For a while I stared out the window, half-asleep. Then I started real-izing that I was hearing mostly the first woman's voice. It was one of those things like a noisy refrigerator, that's been going on a while but you don't notice at first.

What made me tune in wasn't just her voice, it was her saying over and over again how well *she was doing. Then she started saying the same thing about her friends. I gathered that they were a group of wealthy young people in London, going to school or just playing, and she kept repeating it again and again, with the emphasis on that word: "You see, everyone's doing so* well."

By this time, the second woman—who looked like she'd been working all day for peanuts, with a long commute—looked like she was taking a beating. She was hunching into herself, and her smile seemed frozen. Every time she tried to speak, the first woman's voice—she was leaning close now, really face-to-face—overpowered her.

We came to my station. The first woman stood up, too. She said a hearty good-bye, it's been so nice talking to you. The second woman stayed on the train. As I got off I saw that her head was turned to the side, eyes closed. She looked pale, like she was about to cry.

On the platform, the first woman stalked past me. She gave me a quick glance: a sort of guilty look of triumph.

I swear, she knew that I'd seen what had just happened: that I'd watched her steal something, and there was nothing anybody could do about it.

This is probably going to sound silly. I moved into my house two years ago, after my divorce. It was quite a step down from the large tudor house in an exclusive neighborhood. My new house was a much smaller, fifties-style ranch on a nondescript block. I guess I felt sorry for myself and my kids, and thought that adopting two little kittens would make it all seem more like a

home. Once the kittens had gotten used to their new home and grown a little, we naturally started letting them go outside. That's when I met up with my neighbor Ruth.

One of the first days the cats were allowed out I got a call from Ruth, an elderly lady who lived across the street and who, it became evident, spent most of her time staring out her large picture window. Ruth explained in a fussy voice that my cats were scaring away the birds she enjoyed feeding. I politely answered that the cats really enjoyed being outside for short periods and I seriously doubted that two little kittens could do any real damage to the bird population. Still, I put collars with bells on them.

She started calling every day, but now she seemed worried about the cats instead of the birds. Did I know my cats were out? She was afraid they would be hit by a car. She started taking them into her house, feeding them, and then delivering them back to me in person. There would always be a lecture, in that same voice, about how to take care of my cats.

Once winter hit, the calls became more frequent, often twice or three times a day. The minute I let the cats out—they would cry at the front door, dying to get out—she'd call. Of course by now, they'd head straight to her house, for food. She would tell me she was too old to take care of them. I would tell her not to feed them or let them in. Or she would worry that they were too cold. I told her many times—at first politely, and as time wore on, more firmly—that they were well-fed, that I couldn't keep them inside all the time, that they could come back into my house whenever they wanted. She totally ignored all this.

She began hectoring my kids when she saw them outside. She lectured my oldest son about how to care for cats, and told him that his mother obviously didn't love the cats, or she wouldn't let them loose like this. I realized that all of us, the kids and me, were avoiding the front yard, going in and out the back, hurrying from the door to the car.

I started realizing that I was losing my ability to concentrate, when I was working in the house during the day. Some part of me was waiting for that phone to ring, and dreading it. After her call, I would be shaking with rage. I had trouble getting back to what I was doing, and sometimes I could hardly remember what it was. Finally, one day I screamed at her over the phone not to call me any more. She didn't, for another three days, and I felt immense relief. But the calls started again, and she sounded as if nothing had changed.

I've actually stopped answering the phone, screening calls so I won't have to deal with her. I know she's elderly, but she seems totally in control, mentally and physically. I feel like I'm being held hostage by this old woman. I've actually caught myself wishing she would die.

ROAD WARRIORS

Daniel Rhodes notes:

In the immediate area where I live, a small city with rural surroundings and relatively low population, four incidents have been reported in the past twelve months of drivers threatening each other with guns. We're not talking about carjacking, crime, or (obvious) insanity. We're talking about drivers enraged at other drivers.

Getting behind the wheel brings out the beast in many of us, for whatever peculiar reasons. It's worth keeping in mind that at any given time a significant percentage of the world's population is throwing roughly a ton of steel along a road, at speeds that may exceed a mile per minute. And that increasingly, the roads are thronged with people who have no money, no jobs, and no place else to go, but plenty of rage.

Road warriors are increasingly prevalent: not just fast drivers, but emotional vampires with a high degree of awareness. A vehicle provides a perfect vector: powerful, and above all, safe (at least for the emotional vampire). As usual, the *modus operandi* is to pass as though on legitimate business. But the physical destination is not really the point: whether it's the local truck stop or an office, the need for haste is imaginary.

The most likely place to find a road-warrior emotional vampire is in your rearview mirror. There is an overlap with turf emotional vampirism, in that they will typically stake out an area and work it. This may range from deep urban to wide-open freeway.

A classic operation has been described in "A Day in Heck": a stretch of rural or semirural, two-lane road, where speed limits and/or safety considerations constrain most drivers, and passing is difficult or impossible. The road-warrior emotional vampire will know when, and where, police are likely to be around—on any given day, he may make this run a dozen times—and he'll know the road quite well, so driving it fast is no problem. From there, his move is to bear down on the vehicle ahead and harass it, annoying and dangerously distracting the driver.

On the face of it, this is another situation that's apparently random: he is in a hurry to get somewhere and the victim is in his way, or he is a kid playing chicken. But most road-warrior emotional vampires are adults, at least physically (with a preponderance of males, although a growing number of ladies seem to be getting into the act), and telltale signs, like the various maneuvers described, give them away.

There will often be a variant of the vampiric signature. When the victim reaches open road again, or the next slowdown point (a town or stoplight), the road-warrior emotional vampire is likely to either turn off leisurely or, if he has (probably dangerously) passed, to linger ahead and do the same, making sure the victim sees.

Road-warrior emotional vampires tend to fall into two recognizable categories. The first favors older American vehicles, customized, partly trashed, or both. Smoked windshields are common, along with sunglasses and caps. Higher-end road-warrior emotional vampires prefer new, expensive vehicles. In cities, these will often be of foreign make. Enormous, sparkling clean pickup trucks, which have obviously never carried a tool or a scrap of material, are much in vogue in rural areas. Cell phones are a favorite prop.

The body language will tend to be the same: much impatient shifting in the seat, glaring, highly visible exasperation (which may include tricks like flicking headlights), all matched by the agitated movements of the vehicle itself. Related behavior includes bearing down on pedestrians, and the like. Elderly drivers, in particular, may suffer.

Road-warrior emotional vampires present a perplexing problem, with no good defense. Their psychological impact is generally low, but the physical danger they present is significant.

This is one we're all increasingly just going to have to live with.

We'll close this chapter by mentioning one more general phenomenon: the *ripple effect*. It's related to stacking, and can take several forms. In short-term, street-type hits, the immediate hostility aroused by the confrontation may spread to other victims, who also suffer, and who may react with further hostility to others, then or later. In personal relationships, the ripple effect is likely to involve an energy drain on a victim's friends, family, and others concerned about the trouble he's going through.

It can also have more immediate consequences, like the following.

While I was driving in a small city, on a two-lane street with a posted 25 mph speed limit, a car darted out from behind me and passed me rapidly. Immediately ahead was an intersection with a four-way stop. Other vehicles ahead of us were stopped at the intersection. The car that had passed me passed them too, running the stop sign and going through the intersection along with the car just ahead of it.

A pickup truck was waiting at one of the intersecting stop signs. Its driver pulled slowly into the street, blocking all traffic, and jabbed his middle finger, in a "fuck-you" gesture, at the car that had run the stop sign. He stayed there for several seconds, repeating the gesture, apparently oblivious to the other vehicles that still couldn't cross.

5

At Work

Now a huge correspondence began to grow. Sordini inquired how I had suddenly recalled that a land-surveyor shouldn't be summoned. I replied, drawing on Mizzi's splendid memory, that the first suggestion had come from the bureau itself (but that it had come from a different department we had of course forgotten long before this). Sordini countered: why had I only mentioned this official order now? I replied: because I had just remembered it. Sordini: that was very extraordinary. Myself: it was not in the least extraordinary, in such a long-drawn-out business. Sordini: yes, it was extraordinary, for the order that I remembered didn't exist. . . .

As I said, my defense gradually weakened. But whenever Sordini has in his hands even the slightest hold against anyone, he has as good as won, for then his vigilance, energy, and alertness are

actually increased and it's a terrible moment for the victim, and a
glorious one for the victim's enemies.

Franz Kafka, The Castle (1926)

N ow we come to a realm frequented by the next major class of emotional vampire: the merely troublesome (MT).

Street predations may produce intense flare-ups of emotion, but they are almost always short-term, and usually you can walk away.

Not so with your job.

Street predations are also comparatively easy to recognize, if not at the time, then afterward. Work situations tend to be much murkier, for many reasons.

Corporate and bureaucratic structures provide a perfect screen for emotional vampire activity, with much maneuvering taking place behind the scenes. In their own nature, they tend to be impersonally vampiric. An obvious low-level example is committee meetings which drag on endlessly and accomplish nothing, leaving most participants dazed and exhausted.

In general, emotional vampire interactions in the workplace will usually be long-term and subtle. Merely troublesomes are usually quite sophisticated, both in their manipulations and in covering themselves. Rarely will a victim have grounds to confront his predator(s) directly. If he tries, he's likely to end up looking like a fool, and possibly risking his position. One main tenet of emotional vampirism is particularly true in the workplace, and the more so in situations where individual performance is hard to measure: while the victim is devoting the bulk of his time and energy to getting a job done, the emotional vampire is busy maneuvering. He's going to be way ahead.

The type of energy that's desired here is roughly parallel to power in the form of control. There may be an added satisfaction for the emotional vampire, in being the one who is secretly in charge, manipulating people and events behind the scenes.

In this arena, the concrete criteria we suggested in our chapter on "Identification" become particularly useful. Long-term task-blocking is a common syndrome. We are not talking normal business competition: the emotional vampire may not stand to gain materially, and it is likely to happen when the emotional vampire is outwardly working *with* the victim. Probably it will take the victim some time to realize it is going on—and then he will see that it has been, for a while. If you find yourself thinking along the lines of: "If so-and-so put one-tenth as much effort into doing his work as avoiding it, he'd be at the top of his profession"—you may well be in an emotional vampire situation.

Task-blocking will usually be accompanied by oblique, sophisticated turnaround: blaming failures and lack of progress on other people and circumstances. These emotional vampires are adept at spreading blame around nebulously. But if you're the primary victim, a goodly share of it will come to rest, directly or by implication, on you. Very likely, this will be reported to a third party—like your boss—possibly without your knowledge, until the heat starts to come down.

Merely troublesomes in general are adept at diversions, to keep victims off balance, psychologically and emotionally. As we've noted, these will tend to be subliminal: petty irritations the victim may not be consciously aware of, but which gnaw little bites of energy away. They will seem unconscious or random, but they will be repeated in a pattern which upon closer inspection will show to be calculated. Usually, if the victim manages to stop one type, another will spring up. If the victim does happen to be competing with an emotional vampire overtly—for the same goal, or a parallel one—diversions are an almost certain bet.

Inappropriate gifts and unreturnable favors are very likely in the workplace. These can be difficult to distinguish from normal forms of gift-giving: favor-exchanging, expressions of esteem, tokens to make up for conflicts. The timing and motivation of the gifts are important: when and how they are presented; if they seem to follow, or set up, emotional predations—if your sense is that the emotional vampire is, at heart, buying the right to bleed you.

The slicker the emotional vampire, the more oblique these tactics will be.

If the stakes get high, with real consequences—say, after lengthy task-blocking, the work still isn't done and there's no way to cover any longer—the fangs are likely to show. Fearing exposure (and possibly the loss of her job), the emotional vampire may redouble efforts to get rid of anyone who might compromise her. This may include stepped-up turnaround: not simply shifting blame, but twisting events, or even manufacturing them, to discredit the victim. A very telling mark is if a suspected emotional vampire starts defending herself from accusations which no one ever made.

And stay alert for that vampiric signature. In any given round when you've been bested, the emotional vampire is likely to give the boot heel in your ear one more twist.

I met this particular person through a friend. I was told that he shared a similar interest in political goals and ideals and that we could work together as friends on mutual, shared high ideals.

From the beginning, this person was a "task-blocker." He'd give mis-

leading signals about his supposed "huge" interest in politics, but when I tried to work with him, he was always too busy.

Yet, he wanted to "keep in touch" with me because I had valuable ideas and contacts. He'd give me just enough "input" to keep the contact going, but then he'd pull back. He sucked and sucked, sapping my energy and lifeblood. This went on for nine months until I terminated the vampiric association. As with all "bloodsuckers" this relationship pulled me down, while building him up. I became emotionally anemic, while he grew fat like a tick off of my work, my information, my input, and my data. I began having many days of deep depression due to his behavior—crying, confusion, almost feeling like I had no right to pursue the very ideals that I started out with in the beginning!

When I began actively to complain that I was being sapped, used, and fatigued by his unfair behavior, I got the classic "turn around" attack: I had been "pressuring" him. . . . I was to "lay off," although it was he who had represented himself in the beginning as someone so interested in mutual participation. At the end of his attack, he actually had me believing that I was, indeed, at fault! I was a pressurer, an unfair person, etc.

As things progressed, I got the oblique insults—small personalized digs that were invariably couched as "jokes." It was passive-aggressive hostility at its finest. When I'd protest, I'd be told, "I was just joking." Everything was a "joke" to this person.

I strongly believe that his behavior was deliberate. I think it became a game to him, to see how long he could manipulate another person, how long he could suck without being thrown back into the night where he came from and belonged.

To society at large, this person was a pillar of the community. Nobody recognized his "thieving" behavior as anything problematical. By thieving I mean, his constant parasitic taking and taking without giving, his intentional blocking of meaningful action and progress due to his own insecurities, and his bloodsucking behavior.

People should learn to spot these creatures—they are everywhere, particularly in the ranks of those people like to call friends. Drive a stake through their heart at your earlier convenience if you spot the vampire tendency— expose them to sunlight and you'll see them scream, wither, and die.

I've known several people who sound like what you're describing, usually in offices. (Do offices, with their hierarchies, bring this out in people?) The one who comes to mind most, I'll call Susan. She was a pretty, smart, ambitious, extremely organized and efficient woman, who was very hungry for control. She was the secretary, but she essentially ran the office, controlled the boss, and controlled who got what (new computers, for example, went to those she liked; the rest of us suffered with old equipment).

What was it about her? If you called in sick, the tone of her voice was disbelieving. If you gave her a time card with hours on it that you had yet to work, she called you on it. There was absolutely no trust there—and she operated as the office tattle.

Her tone was always flat, dead, long-suffering. She considered herself a martyr. She was unhappy and did not want people around her to be happy. She talked about each person in the office behind their back and she would like to corner you to talk about someone or other who had recently angered her. Then, if I had to give her work, I couldn't just lay it on her desk and disappear, or simply talk to her about it—it was something of a showdown. Didn't I know she was swamped? Did I know this was not a priority? One of the most frustrating things about her was that in these situations work was not simply work, but it was a power struggle.

When I was considerably younger, I worked as a sales assistant at a very toney British clothing store on 57th Street in New York City. I was young, from the Midwest, and quite intimidated by the whole setup. One sweater at this store cost more than my monthly salary. The place had four floors, divided into menswear on the first and second, women's sportswear on the third, and women's expensive coats on the fourth.

Almost all the men and women who worked here had been doing clothing sales their whole lives, and were considerably older than me. I figured they'd hired a few younger people so the place didn't feel like a total mausoleum. Anyway, we worked on salary plus a one percent commission, which doesn't sound like much, but when you're selling a lady from South America three grand worth of cashmere sweaters it adds up. Anyway, I was stationed on the third, women's sportswear floor.

A few months after I was hired, another young woman hit the floor. I'll call her Ann. She was my age, and at first I figured, great, someone to talk to when things are slow, who doesn't just want to show me pictures of her grandchildren. But it didn't take me long to realize that while Ann and I were the same age we were not playing on the same ball field.

Ann, it turned out, lived her whole life on the Upper East Side and was obviously used to money. I couldn't quite figure out what she was doing there; waiting to meet a rich guy, maybe. She latched onto me immediately. She stationed herself next to me on the floor, coordinated our lunch hours, asked me out for drinks after work. I'm thinking, hey, she knows a lot more about this stuff than I do—she told me right away that her last job had been managing a high-end home furnishings place, a position she had to leave because of some weird treachery within the ranks, and the impression she definitely meant to give was that this rag shop was a real comedown for her.

I should describe her. She was incredibly thin and white, with bright red hair, lots of makeup, long nails painted bright red, or sometimes a deep blood-red (no kidding). She was constantly looking in the ten jillion mir-

rors on the floor, checking her hair, makeup. She complained a lot about her weight, which was a total scream, because she was, maybe, a size four. She was striking, I guess you'd say, but not exactly pretty—her nose and lips were really thin, and her eyes were so pale you couldn't really call them blue or grey, they were just no color at all.

Anyway, what I should have seen coming a mile away started to happen—she poached all my sales. We took turns with customers, and if I was up and someone with obvious bucks walked off the elevator, Ann would find a way to get rid of me. She'd let me get a customer in the dressing room, then announce that we had a problem with the cash register, or one of my alterations needed tending to on another floor, any transparent excuse to get me out of there, and then she'd zoom in and close the sale.

Okay. I could handle that. Money is money, and she was more ambitious than me. Except that didn't really seem to be it. I think when she realized I really didn't care much, and wasn't going to fight back, she lost interest. After a while I started to notice that when a customer came in who might come through she wouldn't pay attention, or wouldn't push for the extra accessory that could have netted a few more bucks.

But the poaching wasn't the worst part. My days turned into long, tiring hours of listening to Ann describe, in excruciating detail, her life, which was a lot more interesting than mine, but that fact alone started making me feel smaller and smaller. She would show off her new jewelry, describe the latest stupid thing her boyfriend had done when they were at some exclusive benefit, talk about her incredibly wealthy parents, and how miserable they were trying to find new, creative ways to spend their money. I started to feel like absolutely nothing in my life could compare to what this woman experienced. I was no one.

She also started to discover, or as I now think, create, intrigues in the store. Someone was after her job, or my job, or was sabotaging the entire third floor. She would describe these scenarios in such detail, and with such smarts about the personalities involved, that I would truly believe them, for days on end. Then, suddenly, the person who I was convinced was out to get me, would be having lunch with Ann, and she would kind of wink at me or something as I passed by, and then I'd be in a sweat wondering what the hell was going on now. When I'd try to get a straight answer from Ann, she would laugh. I felt like the dumb kid from the Midwest more than ever.

Luckily, I teamed up with another Minnesota girl, Ginnie, who was hired on the fourth floor about this time. Sometimes one of us would have to float, move around to other floors for days or weeks when they had a staffing problem. Ann was sent up to four for a few weeks, and Ginnie let me know that what had been a fairly smooth sales team on four disintegrated the minute Ann hit. Suddenly Joan and Alice, the two older women who ruled that floor, were at each other's throats. Ginnie was getting the same routine from Ann that I had been through. Thank God we had each other to talk to.

I left the store after a year. Ann wasn't exactly the reason I quit, but she sure figured in to it. I'd started therapy, and my therapist pointed out that I mentioned Ann, or the work situation, fairly often.

Ginnie stayed and moved up to management. She found out that during the time I was there, Ann had frequent meetings with management people, complaining about each and every one of us in great detail. In other words, while she had been giving me advice about who in management was a real jerk, she was having meetings with that jerk where she described my inadequacies as a sales assistant.

It had started to sink in that she wasn't doing this for money, or position in the company. Both those things were added benefits. It was something else: fun, or some kind of power, to see how many hoops I would jump through.

Like I said at the start, I chalked it all up to being naive and not very good at the game. For years, I pretty much forgot Ann.

Fifteen years later, I'm back in the Midwest, coming out of a divorce, *and my first job after many years at home is at an expensive furniture store. I'm no longer a kid, I figure I know how to do this. My first day, I meet two of the three other women on the floor. Everyone's very friendly.*

Day two. The third woman, Michelle, is there. Early thirties, very thin and pale, great clothes, lots of makeup, long nails. As soon as we are introduced, she starts in on a long rant about her lawyer boyfriend, who didn't pay enough attention to her the night before.

Michelle wants to be my friend. Michelle starts giving me confidential information about the boss. Like Ann, Michelle was preoccupied with money, and went through long, complicated explanations, usually about how much she was making on side deals and how much people owed her. I couldn't tell if it was true. She was always broke (although she seemed to have plenty for clothes). Meantime, she's been borrowing from her boyfriend, and she doesn't want him to know she's overdrawn on her checking account. Like a fool, I lend her twenty bucks, which I never saw again.

Before long, Michelle is tripping over herself to steal my customers. The boss starts looking at me funny. I notice that the two other women give Michelle a wide berth. I innocently ask one of them about Michelle and she starts to squirm. She doesn't want to say anything bad, but I get the strong sense that these women are afraid of Michelle.

Déjà vu sets in. I start to see what's happening here, but this time it doesn't seem like a neurotic woman who's latched onto me. It seems like more, maybe because I looked closer.

While this is sinking in, the boss calls me into her office. We had all done inventory the week before. I was teamed with Michelle, who was not only a total time killer, but kept screwing me up in my counts. Then she had to leave early because it was her "anniversary" with her boyfriend. Now the boss wants to know why the numbers don't make sense, and she's talked to Michelle, who swears she tried her hardest but had trouble working with me! I go find the other saleswoman I talked to. She finally hints that she had been through something similar with Michelle. But before I can get the story clear, Michelle is at my side, just like she had radar, and she's reassuring me that the boss is a total creep who always finds someone to blame—and assuring me that she, Michelle, stood up for me.

It was a very weird feeling. It really was like déjà vu: a completely different person, halfway across the country, fifteen years later, but exactly the same situation. Her talking earnestly into my face about how she had backed me up, and me standing there looking back at her. It wasn't even that I just didn't believe what she was saying. It was like I was listening to a tape instead of a person. Very weird stuff.

Here are a few specific phenomena which are common, with merely troublesomes, in work situations.

DORMANT EMOTIONAL VAMPIRISM

Dormant emotional vampirism occurs in relationships which have gone on normally for some time, even years, and then turn vampiric. This can happen in any circumstance, but it's likely when, after relatively smooth going, some form of real pressure—such as competition for a significant goal—comes to bear.

Dormant emotional vampirism is particularly hard to spot, because it's not constant: the victim won't be thinking in those terms. Also, once the situation settles down again, it will probably recede—and the victim will wonder if it really happened (an uncertainty the emotional vampire will probably reinforce).

BOTTLENECKING

Bottlenecking involves task-blocking in ways that are usually unapparent, but may be widespread. An individual maneuvers himself into a position where a lot of traffic must pass through—and then shuts the flow down to a trickle. This will tend to be selective, with victims rotated and/or chosen for their inability to respond. The emotional vampire will be careful not to tangle with any situation that might put him at risk.

A skillful bottleneck emotional vampire can employ a mélange of techniques, like a juggler keeping many balls in the air. These include diversions, and really Byzantine forms of turnaround, with blame for a muddle being shifted onto third, fourth, and fifth parties who might not even know what the issue is about. These situations can go on indefinitely.

VOLATILES AND EXTRA HANDS

A significant step up the vampiric ladder is a more aggressive, and highly recognizable, phenomenon we'll call *volatile emotional vampirism.*

Volatile emotional vampires are usually supervisors or even owners in the business. (If the latter, they're likely to have inherited their position, rather than be the ones who built it originally.) Instead of simply task-blocking, they impair the performance of their staff. Their techniques include studied negligence—not only of their own work, but of matters which spill over to affect everyone—usually accompanied by arrogance, demeaning employees (often publicly), sudden mood shifts and unpredictability, even throwing tantrums—all with the aim of focusing attention, and power, on themselves.

The result is bad feeling, tension, distraction from the work, and general inefficiency. Likely long-term consequences include loss of profit for the business and, ultimately, the loss of employees.

A variation of this, the *extra-hand emotional vampire,* is common in situations where the labor to be done is physical and quantifiable: construction, farming, shop/manufacturing, etc. Like the volatile emotional vampire, the extra hand will be a supervisor or even an owner. His basic premise is that he's a hands-on worker, putting in a full day with the rest of the crew. In fact, he'll only spend a fraction of the day working, although, like the volatile, he'll make sure he's highly visible (and audible) when he's there. The rest of his time will be spent, essentially, goofing off: either outright (at a bar playing the poker machines) or obliquely (making a dozen unnecessary trips to a supplier).

This in itself might not be serious (and can even be a plus: most crews are delighted to have supervisors like this out of the way). Problems arise because the extra hand is figuring his own work time into the production schedule, when in fact there's one less body doing the work. What actually gets done therefore keeps falling short of what is needed to remain on schedule.

Since he's in charge, and/or the liaison to superiors, the blame is going to come down on the rest of the workers, with increased pressure and even threats of job loss. As with volatiles, the atmosphere will be charged with tension and bad feeling. In these situations, there is the additional danger that this creates a good breeding ground for physical injury.

Astonishingly, volatile and extra-hand emotional vampires, like most merely troublesomes, have a way of landing on their feet—leaving behind their former employees, the losers in the situation.

Several years ago I took a part-time job as a proofreader for a small press. I had no problem getting hired, although I had had no real professional experience. They were willing to teach me to use the standard marks and all that. As I found out, their turnover was pretty high.

The staff was almost all young people except the big boss, who was about sixty. He'd been a college professor, and he had that glower that some teachers really get off on using with students: like you're on trial, and they can make things miserable for you if they feel like it.

I noticed right off that the place seemed—quiet isn't exactly the right word—subdued, like everybody was walking on eggshells. There were three or four other proofreaders. We worked in a separate room and weren't considered part of the regular staff, so we were cut off from the main office interaction.

But within a day or two, I heard the boss's voice raised, reading somebody out. It was the kind of tone that chills you: not just loud and angry, but with something savage in it. You hear out-of-control parents use it to their kids sometimes, and you want to take the kids away from them.

Over the next weeks I started realizing that everyone lived in terror of the guy. It was like he spent most of his time prowling the halls, or lurking half-hidden, waiting to jump on somebody. The first time it happened to me, I had xeroxed some papers and left an original in the machine: one sheet of paper, twenty feet down the hall from where I worked. For this, he blew up at me for a good half-minute. He was right in my face, and I still remember exactly how he looked: glittering eyes, face bright red, spitting flecks.

I should mention that his girlfriend, about thirty years younger, worked as the office manager. She never said much, but there was a very definite sense that she was his sidekick, feeding his ego, even singling people out for punishment. It was clear that they were a team, more or less against every-body else. Except that fairly often, they would give big, expensive parties, and then they were everyone's best friend.

Two or three afternoons a week, he'd hold a staff meeting. The proof-readers didn't go, but we could hear him through a couple of walls. These meetings would last two hours and sometimes longer, and he'd be talking the whole time: bursts of ranting, then long silences, then more ranting.

Afterward, the staff people would come out looking like zombies. Then, almost always, he would sort of make the rounds, slapping people on the back and joking with them—like they had had a big problem that required some unpleasantness, but now it was cleared up and everything was okay.

But when I got to know some of them a little, I found out that nothing ever did get cleared up in those meetings: no business or even real complaints. They were just a forum for him to rave. There was also a feeling that the more efficient you were, the more likely he was to come down on you, and if you had a good idea, he would sideline it. Like he was jealous.

I found out, too, that the press, which had been a solid, prestigious little operation for many years, was falling into financial trouble. It was easy to see why: he never seemed to do any work himself, just stopped everyone else from doing theirs. Plus people's time and energy were cut in half by those meetings, and the general unhappiness.

I quit before too long. A couple of years later I heard that the press had folded. He and his girlfriend landed on their feet, got good jobs in the university system.

ARTFUL DODGING

This one lies in a midrange between large-scale corporate vam-pirism and the more personal predations which are our main concern. But it is common enough to bear mentioning; and this type of emotional vampire will often engage in other tactics.

Ideal situations for this lie at management level, where there's no immediate accountability in terms of performance. There are many permutations. Small, loosely knit associations, with a central director or coordinator working unsupervised, are especially vulnerable (more especially if they are nonprofit, with much of the labor volunteer). The artful dodger may also appear as a consultant, or independent expert for hire, in some field.

As soon as he feels secure in his position, he will start cutting corners. We're not talking about actual embezzlement (although he is likely to pay himself well for work he hasn't done and even time he hasn't spent), just sloppiness and increasing chaos. He'll probably be extremely skilled at covering himself. With no one checking, this can often be prolonged indefinitely.

When he knows the noose must start to tighten, he'll bail, well ahead of time. It's usually easy for him to find another, similar job, because his credentials will still look good. By the time the mess is discovered, he'll be long gone—possibly in another geographical area and/or situation where it's never likely to catch up. In these cases, the victims (including the organization in general) are whoever has to clean up the mess. In addition to the trouble itself, they may also inherit the bad reputation their predecessor has engendered, while he gets away scot-free.

Vampiric signatures, such as squeezing final perks from the organization as he's leaving, are common.

If an artful-dodger emotional vampire does get caught in his own game, look for major turnaround.

I had been working part-time, two years, for a community service organiza-tion, when Trudy was hired on as director. I didn't resent her coming in as my boss, and I hadn't applied for the job; I have a family and was still in graduate school, so I didn't want the added hours.

She revealed various things about herself to me in the next two years we worked together. I credited her with a pretty keen intelligence; she was edu-cated and knowledgeable. I took a business roadtrip with her once, where she pointed out everything along the way from the geological to the astronomical. I was impressed, then, by her apparent grasp of various worlds. It seemed she could discuss anything.

I also realized soon after our working relationship began that she was excessively talkative, soaking anything from the mundane to the complex in a flood of words. Taken apart, her thoughts would have been tolerable; everything she said was clear enough. But when she spoke, the air became inflated with words. I remember feeling caught once she took off in a con-versation, knowing that, because she barely stopped for breath, I'd have no chance to extricate myself. Needless to say, I avoided conversations with her because I felt completely drained afterward.

She sought confrontation. She and I were the only employees; as such, we dealt with business people and community members throughout the city. Within a month after we began working together, I realized that we were "bickering" with someone almost all the time. One week it might be the xerox repairman; the next round could involve someone in a neighboring office, a restaurant down the street, a local bar, an out-of-town caller. On a few occa-sions, we battled with someone who was key to a project we were working on. Once, over a "personality conflict" between Trudy and another woman, we lost a chance for improving and strengthening our organization.

In the years previous to Trudy's arrival, I only remember a couple of minor problems in our dealings with others. Now, my working hours seemed to always include outrage, and I began to notice that I was never out from under Trudy's intense preoccupation with going over and over again the thoughtlessness of others.

I discovered at this time that she was a liar—the most dangerous kind. Her lies were hooked to enough truth to pass the tests of simple inquiry. To make certain that she (or "we") stood "wronged" she invented "events" that had never occurred—phone calls she claimed she made that were never received, arguments she recounted in "telling" detail that had never happened. I had learned the hard way to be as silent as possible around her. If I uttered anything related to her tirades, she took my words and wove them in with her own explanations to others as a way of securing the credibility of her arguments. Her "victims," I believe, were befuddled, hit by a quick, deft shove that left them half in the dark and probably questioning themselves rather than her. She emerged from these incidents victorious, always.

I was the only person who worked alongside Trudy; everyone else involved with the organization worked outside of our offices. Our employers avoided questioning Trudy's actions. I remember jokes about her "long-winded" (and unnecessary) phone calls. They seemed troubled when we lost the account I spoke of above, but after looking into it, they came away uncertain about where the trouble began. There was rarely the suggestion that Trudy's "habits" represented any danger.

In truth, I never directly questioned her either, even though she knew that I knew of her lies and deceptions. I think she began to see me as somewhat of a compatriot because I knew about the goings-on behind her schemes and yet stood silently by. She was technically my boss, and I needed the job. I grew to detest working hours, however, and when I tried to articulate and to share with anyone else my perception of this woman, I felt a little ridiculous and open to the notion that I was somehow being petty about her behavior.

I began to believe that Trudy could convince anyone of anything. I also knew, without a doubt, that at some point I would be the target of her strange and unpredictable outrage.

And I was. One afternoon, Trudy informed me, in the course of several thousand words, that our employers were unhappy with my work. She implied that I might be fired. She suggested that only her defense of me had saved my job.

I should have known, then, that Trudy had invented the entire incident. She had not received any such communication from the people I worked for. The entire story had sprung from a harmless comment one of them made to Trudy about my working up to the last minute on a report.

I was doing so because Trudy had assured me she would take care of it. But when I came to the office the day before it was due, the report was a mess and she had left town. I won't go on about this part of it, but one of the reasons I'd gotten down about the job was just this sort of thing: she'd insist on doing particular things—actually keep me from them, when I offered—and then a situation would come up where she couldn't finish, and I'd end up racing to turn out a hasty, poor product. She went out of town a lot, on trips that weren't business related, but she always paid herself full salary. She also put in a lot of "overtime"—which in fact meant that she was hanging out at the office, half-living there, because her apartment was a mess—and she'd pay herself comp time for that.

I don't want to go on either about the overall effect on me and my family. There were times I really thought I was losing my mind. My husband grew up in a small ranching and mining community, and is very straightforward. I honestly believe that if Trudy had been a man, there would have been violence.

In the years I'd worked for this organization, the quality of my work had never been questioned. In truth, my enthusiasm had ebbed over the twenty months I'd worked alongside Trudy. I realize now that she had detected the drop in my commitment to a business she'd come to see as her own. I think she found that unacceptable. I've often wondered what reaction she anticipated from me at that moment. I think she felt I'd cower and be *grateful for her support. Maybe she thought our working relationship from then on would be more to her liking, with me in a clear, subordinate position of gratitude for her show of loyalty to me.*

My response may have alarmed her. I walked out. I quit.

By the time I reached home, I decided to confront my employers. I felt they owed me their own explanations and that they should face me with any discontent over my work.

In the meantime, Trudy had called each of them individually with a reconstruction of the conversation she and I had had. She had to cover her tracks and cast doubt on anything I might say to them.

By the time I spoke with each one of them, their reaction felt familiar. They were confused; none of them had ever expressed dissatisfaction with me, but by the time I reached them, I think they had begun to wonder if they should have questioned or examined my work sooner. I got the impression that they thought I had reacted emotionally to a mere suggestion Trudy had made. I was in a defensive position—over an invented scenario that they half-believed had occurred. There was no way to explain the deeper truth, or about all that had gone on before. As I said, the incident felt familiar. Still, I was extremely careful not to say too many negative things about Trudy.

She stayed on as director. I kept working for the organization freelance, but never with Trudy again. After several more months, our employers quietly asked me to come back. I gathered that some other odd things had come to light. Trudy resigned, although she got glowing references.

Since that time, she and I have come to share two mutual friends. Both these women have made it clear to me that I overreacted; they like Trudy very much.

I've taken to saying nothing negative about her again.

TEAMS

Emotional vampire teams are probably more common in the work-place than in public or personal relationships, although they exist in all social areas.

Secretary-boss operations are time-honored, and take many forms. Often, the boss engages in a more serious type of emotional vampirism (such as volatilism), with the secretary assisting, taking an energy cut, and perhaps running sidelines.

Another common situation—especially with a victim who is new on the scene—is for a co-worker to give assurances that it's permissible (or unnecessary) to do something. A higher-up then reprimands the victim sternly. As is often the case, besides the bad feeling and confusion, there's a spin-off: the victim is put in the unhappy position of either swallowing the blame, or snitching.

Numerous other variations occur, usually under the guise of power alliances and struggles.

Occasionally, two emotional vampires will stage a disagreement in order to draw in a victim. Further techniques can then come into play: besides those we've described, Loyalty Tests are common (see chapter 6, "Up Close"). The victim's best bet here is to withdraw, if possible, and let them fight it out. If they are real emotional vampires, they won't quarrel—with each other—for long.

This experience began innocently enough. I got a phone call requesting an estimate to remodel a bath. I've been a remodeling contractor for twenty-five years in a small city—such calls are routine.

I went to the clients' home. Brad and Laura were the type of prospective client I had begun to see more and more frequently: midthirties, high-end professionals whose jobs were clearly well-paying but somehow never defined, children "part of the picture" but actually always out of the picture (off somewhere else in their 5,000-square-foot house), beautiful, healthy, seemingly guileless people with a tendency toward phrases like "we want the whole package" and when can "your people" start.

They wanted very high-end stuff. They would see photos in House Beautiful.

I worked up a bid. Total cost was $18,500 for labor and materials. I am not a good businessman, I don't ever really include substantial profit when I figure. I just try to cover my time and that of the skilled people who, over the years, I have learned will do more than a good or acceptable job— they'll do a great job. I've always approached each project as if my life depended on it. I've always been willing to eat time, and to in fact work for free for extended periods if that was what it took to bring a job in on time, on my agreed figure, and to the customer's satisfaction. In this I am no different than any other honest person, and contrary to popular opinion, there are a multitude of small, independent contractors who are exactly like me. Brad and Laura, and I think they knew this from the start, had hit on the ideal victim.

Before I began the job, I warned them, as I always do clients, that it would be disruptive and messy. I told them I'd do my best, with plastic tarps and shop vacs, to minimize the upheaval. I also warned them that while most of the job would be finished within the specified time, delays are in the nature of this work—materials aren't always immediately available, the weather turns bad, an emergency arises somewhere else for myself or a subcontractor—and there'd probably be details that would string out after the completion date. They said fine to it all. I began.

My first indication of trouble came when two of my much-preferred subs, upon hearing of who this project was for, suddenly backed out. They didn't tell me why, but I knew it had something to do with the clients. Their withdrawal forced me to scramble to find replacements.

The initial stages were difficult. The floor had to be jackhammered to move drain lines, and the wall dividing the bathroom from the bedroom, still occupied by the owners, had to be removed. Some time within the first few days of starting, I heard Laura loudly exclaiming over the phone that "they've torn the whole place up, and my god, there are chunks of debris everywhere—it's a nightmare!" The call was not in humor or jest. I swear she looked right at me when she wailed this. I was on the defensive from the get-go, and I'm the kind of person who can't bear to feel responsible for another's unhappiness—another thing I think, looking back, that she sensed. We worked double-hard to contain the mess, but her angry laments grew more shrill daily.

I was worried—several thousand dollars in, which to me is a lot of money—but the work itself was going fine. Imagine my surprise when one day, coming in from bidding another job, I found that she had directed my crew to demolish the second bathroom on that floor. There had not been anything about this in the plans. In practice, especially remodels, jobs almost always involve extra work than what is contracted for, and almost always, clients are reasonable about paying for it. I started to say something to that effect, but she looked right at me and said—as always, in a voice charged with emotion— "As long as you're destroying half the house, you might as well do the rest." She also made it clear that she and her husband were going to suffer agonizing inconvenience because now they had to climb a flight of stairs to use a bathroom. Like a fool, I let it go, allowing myself to think we'd settle it later.

It's important to realize (though I did not at the time) that Laura was not crazy. She was a highly competent professional who was very good at her job (co-owner, with her husband, of an accounting firm). Her work life never skipped a beat. But, it was clear by now, her personal life and the sanctity of her home were utterly, and maliciously, violated by me and my crew. I started to feel like I was walking on eggs, hunched over, like I'd been skinned. I lived in fear of daily exchanges that went like: "My god, you mean that window won't go in until next week*? Oh, my god. Oh, Brad is just going to lose it when he hears this." My crew, men who'd been with me ten years or more, were ready to mutiny.*

Away from work, in my own home, I was overwhelmed with guilt. Now that I had two bathrooms to do, my schedule—for other jobs, too—was shot. I began to doubt whether I would get paid. I began to lie awake nights worrying, trying to figure out how to work faster—just to get it done.

The project had now expanded into the hall and guest bedroom, again without my directly authorizing it. Laura would simply demand that my men do something, always when I wasn't around. By now I'd made it clear that I expected to be paid for the extra work. They never exactly agreed— instead, they took an aggressive tone, and said that since the house was so disrupted anyway, we might as well fix the other things. I finally realized that what they meant was, since we had torn up their house, we owed it to them to do a bunch of extra work free.

That was when Brad started his work. One day he confronted me with the news that a painter had told him I was "the worst contractor in town." As I said, I've been working in the same small city for twenty-five years; if I wasn't any good, I'd have long since been out of business. I was so taken aback that I didn't realize the obvious odd thing: the painter had done some work for them (hired by Laura, not by me; I hardly knew him), and Brad had complained continually, to me, about his work. Now he was using that same painter to criticize mine. That night I called the painter and asked him if it was true. He denied ever saying anything like it.

I then called Brad and Laura and offered to withdraw from the project, that they were obviously dissatisfied, and I wasn't right for the job. I told them I'd help find another contractor to finish it. They both—to my amazement, although I was on such an emotional waterslide by then, nothing seemed strange—assured me that no, no, they had complete confidence in me, etc.

I tried to sort through the facts. Both of them complained endlessly about the work, especially about the added time involved—and yet, on a daily basis, they were directing my crew or subs to do significant extra work— wallpapering one room, rewiring another, changing the hot water heater, on and on. I started to see that their routine was clearly calculated: keeping us psychologically on the defensive, and using that to demand further concessions, a process that could go on indefinitely.

Needless to say, by now I was really worried about money. I was right. We held a meeting. They complained about the work in every detail, questioned each bill in emotionally charged voices, actually used terms like, "How dare you submit a bill in such and such an amount," which, of course, was only industry standard. I offered, for by now the third time, to withdraw. Once again, their tone changed quickly: they had full confidence in me, but needed to express "their feelings."

It went on and on. Brad ordered a custom, glass-doored cabinet, which I clearly told him would be above the bid-projected price, and when it arrived, with a (very reasonable) bill for $800, actually shouted at me that I must be in cahoots with other tradesmen to charge such prices. Laura accused my men of deliberately dumping plaster dust in a closet, and screamed, "Do you hate me so much you're trying to ruin my clothes, too?"

My life had become a waking nightmare. I was terrified both of financial disaster and slander. I couldn't sleep. My children asked their mother what was wrong with Dad. I was literally sick. Every time I saw some glimmer of hope, they would swiftly, with uncanny ability, spot it and find a way to crush it. I was no longer sure of anything. When you're on the defensive like that, you lose all sense of proportion. I started fantasizing about death, about my family collecting my life insurance and being all right, about what a cool, refreshing drink it would be.

Finally Laura, literally pointing a screwdriver at me with a trembling hand, informed me that she could not "live with" the countertop, which had

arrived unmarred from the factory, and she had seen installed. It was
formica. She wanted it replaced with a more expensive surface, maybe
marble: I could work out the extra cost with Brad.

I realized that besides the money I'd never see, it meant at least another
week of work—the sink and mirrors had been installed, too—and that
after it, another problem, and then another, would arise. I never said a
word. I packed my tools and left. I walked into my house and told my wife
I'd just lost 7500 bucks. I spent many evenings and weekends after that,
working to try to keep our debts manageable, but it was the best money I ever
spent. It may just have bought me my life.

But it's hard to leave it at that. It was all the bullshit that went with
it, the sneaky way they jacked me around. They knew I drove an old truck,
barely made ends meet, that I lacked business sense, that I loved my wife and
kids—that I could be taken advantage of out of fear and desperation. I'm
starting to see that the world is full of those people now. I'm wary in a way
I was never raised to be.

ELICITORS AND ENABLERS

The workplace is prime territory for a peculiar type of emotional
vampire we might call an *elicitor.* She often operates by more sophisticated variations of the "Let's you and her fight" theme.

Elicitors are the chameleons of emotional vampires. They will
subtly advise others to take stances, and risks, rarely doing so themselves, then fade from sight during battle or serious work. When it's
over, they reappear. If there is triumph, they claim to have been on
that side all along; if failure, they were against it from the start.

Elicitors are also skilled at engineering and prolonging interpersonal conflicts, sometimes among many people.

A variation with a different orientation, but which can have similar results, involves emotional vampire enablers. Enablers facilitate emotional vampire operations, usually unwittingly, and often with genuinely good intentions.

ACTUALLY DANGEROUS IN THE WORKPLACE

Actually dangerous (AD) emotional vampirism in the workplace is likely in situations which are highly charged emotionally, such as when there are ties that are strong in themselves (a victim falls in love with an AD boss or co-worker), or when a career is at stake, and the actually dangerous is in a position to make or break an underling.

These are among the most difficult of situations, with material and emotional factors compounding each other.

COMBAT

A word on combat specific to the workplace is in order. These tend to be serious fights, which cannot be ignored: they involve one's success, keeping the job itself, and/or peace of mind while doing it. Launching a defense will probably require much effort and skill, and will cost the victim considerable energy, no matter what.

But there are factors on the victim's side. Emotional vampires encountered at work are not likely to have a powerful emotional hold, like those in personal life (although there may be overlap). Unlike on the street, victims have time to think things over.

Best bet, as usual, is to recognize what's happening—one thing that's certain is that the emotional vampire will be at a great advantage if you don't—and then start trying to outmaneuver. While merely troublesomes tend to be extremely crafty, and capable of amazing refinement and creativity, their overall tactics are limited. If you know what the moves are likely to be, you will be better able to counter them swiftly and effectively, or even foresee and block them. Be prepared for a chess game—or running dogfight—that may last months or years.

It's sadly possible that victims may run up against an emotional vampire who, because of seniority, or tenacity, or simply corporate inertia, will succeed in overcoming.

6

Up Close

The vampire is prone to be fascinated with an engrossing vehemence, resembling the passion of love, by particular persons. In pursuit of these it will exercise inexhaustible patience and stratagem, for access to a particular object may be obstructed in a hundred ways. It will never desist until it has satiated its passion, and drained the very life of its coveted victim. But it will, in these cases, husband and protract its murderous enjoyment with the refinement of an epicure, and heighten it by the gradual approaches of an artful courtship. In these cases it seems to yearn for something like sympathy and consent.

J. Sheridan LeFanu, *Carmilla* (1872)

Until now, we have been dealing for the most part with emotional vampirism in which—although material and psychological consequences can be significant—the personal and emotional hold of these predators on the victim isn't strong.

When that becomes the case, emotional vampirism may escalate into a much more serious realm. We will use the term *personal emotional vampirism* to describe this more dangerous predation.

Here, the emotional vampire goes for the throat in terms of the desired energy: the most vulnerable emotions with damage which in extreme cases may threaten mental and physical health, and even life itself. Needless to say, this is where the actually dangerous (AD) vampire is most likely to be found.

This arena is also by far the most complex, and some aspects of it verge on the sacrosanct. Our treatment in general has been necessarily superficial, and at times semihumorous. We think that this is appropriate for the emotionally removed situations we have been discussing. But close relationships that experience serious trouble are matters for deep consideration, compassion, and professional counseling. Our scope is very limited here; we mainly try to point out a few ways of recognizing whether an individual might be victim in an emotional vampire friendship or romance.

Although one of our tenets is that emotional vampirism must be conscious at least to some degree, in personal relationships this is most likely to get blurred. A great deal of it is not intentionally destructive. Particularly in long-standing relationships, the emotional vampire may consider his or her emotional demands to be legitimate, or manage not to notice the effect they have—as if the predator, like the victim, is subject to mind-clouding.

These situations are also especially tough because there is usually real affection involved, which may be intense and lifelong. It is very difficult to separate the vampiric element, let alone to neutralize it. Many people are willing victims to those they care about.

Really conscious, AD predators—those who move in on victims, make concerted efforts to establish an emotional hold, and then drain them to a life-threatening extent—are rare. They *do* exist, usually as extremely manipulative and unscrupulous individuals who are, however, likely to be attractive, charming, and almost certainly will possess great personal magnetism. They are by far the most clever and resourceful of emotional vampires, and victims may not recognize that they have even been in such a relationship until years after it is over (or for that matter, ever). Material control or demands—money, influence, sex—often overlap with the emotional bond.

In some esoteric thought, a further level is recognized: highly conscious psychic vampires, the closest counterparts to their legendary brothers. Their predations are calculated to be destructive and even deadly. They sap a victim's life force as directly as possible in a conscious attempt to prolong their own lives or to gain power.

We will concentrate, as usual, on everyday situations, and we should make a somewhat fine distinction: personal emotional vampirism may not involve intentional harm; however, the drain on the victim, and the potential consequences, can be extremely serious since there tends to be a close emotional bond, and because the emotions involved are particularly strong. Thus, personal emotional vampirism tends to lie near the borderline between the merely troublesome variety and the actually dangerous, and it can swing either way with circumstances.

Some of the phenomena we have discussed—like the ripple effect that damages friends and family as well as the victim—may be particularly acute in the personal arena. We'll also note that many situations may be either active or passive: another reason for personal emotional vampirism's complexity. In practice, there tend to be complex degrees of elicitation, consent, and mutual draining.

I have an aunt that seems to get everyone stirred up in the family from time to time. She swoops into our lives every three to four years and comes in looking so perky and wonderful. However, she has a way of making the people around her feel smaller. I have noticed this since I was a small kid. I would seem to lose my emotional energy after interacting with her. I communicated this to my wife and sister and her husband and told them I was going to do a test the next time she came to town. (By the way, they all felt the same way about her.)

So . . . she was in town last May for a wedding in the family. I greeted her with a cordial hello but the whole time I held my arms across my stomach as if I was not letting her get to my insides. I avoided her for the next three days, only giving her very short answers to her questions and then leaving her presence very quickly. I would act as if I had to go to the bathroom, get a drink, etc., etc. . . . It drove her crazy! She just kept coming at me even to the point of inviting herself down to my house for a visit. I refused the visit on the grounds that we were getting to bed early that night but she persisted to the point that she said "expect me, I am coming." I told her to call first because the guard dogs would be out and that was it . . . she never mentioned a word after that. I am convinced. She got zero of my energy this time. There is something to this theory.

My husband and I had two roommates (I'll call her M and her son, R), who lived with us off and on for several years. She tried to make herself

indispensable in our lives. We met before my children were born and she always "seemed" pleasant and very helpful. We shared the common bond between women . . . and that was good, since we had my husband's male friends hanging around and also a male roommate. For a long time I thought she was my friend and I never attributed the chaos in our lives to be generated by her. M never could maintain a job as a cleaning woman or her own place to live . . . and as R got older he became a troubled teen. Our friendship dissolved when she and her son were fighting and swearing in front of my toddler and they wouldn't stop. My anger escalated and finally threw them out of our house and lives.

The very interesting thing was that another person described what she saw in my relationship with M. This other person had had an accident with a head injury that left her able to see auras. She had never come forward to tell me because I appeared to value my friendship with M. Anyway she told me after M was gone that she saw a black tether or rope of negative energy connecting M and I and that it wrapped around me as if to encase me in darkness/blackness. I had always thought that the frustration my husband felt regarding M was because she feigned helplessness when dealing with men. I can see now how she would use that to get close to people while seeming very small and powerless, soft-spoken, never raising her voice. She was kind of seductive in that way. All her relationships that I knew of ended badly where she would be kicked out of a living situation or dumped by a boyfriend. People always reacted very angrily to her which always seemed out of proportion to her "seeming" powerlessness and soft-spokenness.

As I look back on my life in the past ten years or so, I can see patterns of relationships that take much more from me and my husband than we ever get back. I've been trying to define the fine line between compassion and doormat, trying to halt the constant stream of people that come into our lives to take whatever we have, be it energy, money, possessions, dinner . . . whatever, without ever giving an equal amount back. It seems that as soon as we rid ourselves of one or more people, one or more enter. Nature abhorring a vacuum, if you will.

Well, I guess it's nice to know that someone, somewhere, believes this to be true. It would be nice, as well, if you could tell me a way to protect myself. Right now I feel as if one or two people I know kind of suck the energy right out of my life although it doesn't feel malicious. It's almost as if they don't know how to survive any other way. It's pretty hard to keep myself focused in my daily duties as a wife and mother, much less motivate myself to return into the workforce, even though that's what I really want to do.

If anyone involved with this book has any information on how to stop this weird pattern I believe I/we are in, I would be most grateful for some assistance. Perhaps a spell, amulet, ritual . . . exorcist? I'll buy the book anyway, as this is great information to have and share.

Thanks . . . for giving me the opportunity to look at my situation in a new way.

And good luck.

When someone in my family was diagnosed as terminally ill, Aunt Sadie came to stay to provide help and support during the crisis. After several such deaths, the sons and daughters of the deceased discovered that jewelry, antiques, hand-made quilts, and other valuable items belonging to their parents had disap-peared. Attention had been focused on dealing with grief, loss, and funeral arrangements; these other losses were not discovered until several weeks later. Indeed, it took years for the cousins to compare notes and to eventually realize that the common denominator in all these events was Aunt Sadie.

Sometimes she would wear a dress easily recognized as having belonged to the deceased. When asked by the family members, she would emphatically state that it was a gift from her ailing departing sister.

The loss of these sentimental and valuable items created a great deal of turmoil among the survivors. Asking Aunt Sadie about the missing items would have seemed ungrateful, and there was no concrete proof that she had taken them.

Is this the kind of thing you mean by emotional vampires?

THE VAMPIRE AS SEDUCER

In our Introduction, we noted that emotional vampire predations in public and in the workplace are more likely to resemble rape than seduction. The personal arena is where the two blend together into another gray area, where emotional vampirism gets blurred with affection.

The classic vampire has often been presented in literature and drama as a master (or mistress) of seduction. In several prominent stage and film versions, Dracula has been played primarily as the ultimate womanizer. All his victims—even, especially, angelic women like Mina Harker—yield to his mysterious power. (Overall, there has been an interesting tendency to make the vampire figure pleasing: from the gory, nonhuman monster of older cultures, to the foul, reeking, brutal—but human—animated corpses of just a few centuries ago, to the cultured aristocrat of Dracula and spin-offs. Increasingly, the modern forms seem entirely human, often attractive, and in most ways rather ordinary, except for their need for blood. It is also noteworthy that modern vampires may be portrayed as incapable of having physical sex. Bloodsucking, described in erotic terms, replaces it.)

It's arguable that the more power the victim willingly yields—as opposed to the emotional vampire's acquiring it forcibly—the more serious the consequences are likely to be, and that this in itself may be a nascent form of vampirism. Many people probably know individuals who get victimized again and again, even in physically dangerous ways, seeming to seek it out.

This may be the origin of the legend that the vampire's bite turns victims into vampires themselves.

SEXUAL VAMPIRISM

This topic in itself is so vast, complex, and emotionally loaded, we can hardly even pretend to scratch the surface. We will just suggest a few basic measures of whether a particular type of sexual manipulation may involve emotional vampirism. The tactics are similar to other forms: initial behavior that causes unhappiness, ways of extending the tension, diversions, turnaround, and so on.

A few preliminary points:

We are talking about sexually oriented relationships in general, and the emotional interactions that accompany them, not just physical sex.

By no means can all sexual manipulation be labeled vampiric. There are all kinds of other reasons and all degrees of emotional vampirism mixed in with other, often positive, emotions.

Types of manipulation with vampiric elements will probably involve the victim's sense of being used. What is at stake may clearly be power or control, at the cost of the victim's unhappiness and emotional energy. Other tactics may enter in: disparagement, general or specifically sexual; the emotional vampire hinting or even making clear that he's having other affairs; aggression or suspect timing with emotional or sexual demands—when the victim is weakened, distracted, or otherwise off balance; etc. Emotional, economic, physical, or other means may be used to prevent the victim from ending the relationship.

A more passive variation involves one partner withdrawing emotionally or sexually, for reasons which are oblique or unspecified, but which the emotional vampire makes subtly clear are the victim's fault. This may take the form of frequent unhappiness, picking fights over nothing, etc. Affection may return as unpredictably as it was withdrawn, followed by a blissful interlude. After the victim has yielded up sufficient energy, the emotional vampire will be charged to a level that prompts him to reinforce the bond, to achieve future manipulation and gratification.

Extreme cases may involve the "I can't live without you" syndrome (the flip side of an active emotional vampire forcibly and abusively continuing a relationship): if the victim tries to sever the tie, the emotional vampire's attachment becomes desperate, possibly with self-destruction threatened or even attempted. Emotional vampires of this sort may also be prone to sickness or injuring themselves physically. These situations are particularly distressing: the victim is himself miserable, it's clear that he's the source of his partner's misery, and yet he doesn't dare leave.

In either active or passive forms, the victim may recognize warning signals of an approaching episode, which he has come to dread. He may expend great energy trying to stave off his partner's advances or withdrawal, usually without success. The emotional cost will probably mount (a form of stacking and/or ripple effect), with his frustration spilling out into other areas of his life. Consequences can get serious.

There can be several outcomes, including: the emotional vampire discarding the drained victim and moving on to another; the victim ending the relationship and emerging more or less intact; the two remaining together, perhaps forming a team to draw in other victims.

In some instances of sexual vampirism, there seems to be a drain of physical vitality by one partner from another. Many people have probably witnessed this in some form; again, whether it's purely psychological or an actual energy exchange must remain a judgment call.

A common theme in bawdy stories throughout history has been of an aging man who takes a younger spouse and gets physically exhausted by her demands, and/or cuckolded. But there are individuals, of either sex, for whom this seems to work the other way around: who pointedly take younger lovers as they themselves age, sometimes in series, and maintain exceptional vitality. (Casanova admitted cheerfully that this was his M.O.) Emotional drain, and even premature aging or illness, may settle in on the younger partner—who may then be discarded for someone new.

It has often been noted that nymphomania in the clinical sense does not involve women who enjoy sex and are seeking pleasure. On the contrary, they are viewed as unhappy and sexually uncomfortable, but use this as a way of trying to achieve emotional fulfillment.

As someone who occasionally indulges in reading self-help books, and laments the rarity of those who provide interesting insights and amusement, I was intrigued by your e-mail concerning vampires. If I may, I would like to submit a few comments that do not constitute a personal story, but some conceptual concerns.

There seem to be people for whom "emotional vampire" is a good epitaph. However,

1. It should be emphasized that these are not simply people who make noise a lot and make you tired at the end of a workday. It seems to me that the extreme title of "vampire" should be reserved for a special kind of people who seem to "destroy everything they touch" emotionally. The following situations come to mind:

A professor (or a cult-leader, such as Ayn Rand in her lifetime) looks younger than she is, all her advisees/disciples look older than they are. She drives them to drink not only with the amount of work she gives them, but with the amount of emotional energy they invest in pleasing her and being "good enough" for her strict norms. As they shrivel, she seems to flourish, with the help of their admiration as well as perhaps using them.

A man has relationships with women to whom he gives little and from whom he takes all he can get. Perhaps he likes women to be younger than himself, so he can somehow, in an unclear way, "absorb" some of their energy. The relationship is always very "serious" and intense for her, but not so for him, and when he breaks up, she experiences a devastation that expresses itself in a feeling of being exhausted, depleted of all the things that she has given. (I think Lord Byron the poet was a lot like that.)

If the legend of the vampire has roots in human psychology/gossip, I would bet these are the kinds of interactions that the legend is based on: these people seem to thrive on interactions that drain others, not simply doing things that drain others. They "feed" on {the emotional} "blood" from other people. I am sure you have a well-developed typology of vampires that I am not aware of, but all I want to say here is that one should be careful not to extend the concept of vampire too much. Many people now think that the word "codependence" does not mean much, because it is used too broadly to include any interpersonal problem under the sun.

2. It seems to me that it is too simplistic to say that vampires, however you define them, have the "intention" of stealing energy. First of all, not all vampires are the same. Second, it seems clear that some vampires are not aware that they are vampires—that vampirism as a life-strategy can easily be developed as unconsciously as many others. At any rate many vampires don't go around thinking "let's see how much energy I can get out of this person," but just think, "what a lovely girl," "what a cool person to work with." They have no insight into the vampiric nature of their interaction with people. They might easily think they are just misunderstood and deep down inside they are great guys/gals. You and I may be vampires and not know it—think that we ask others for favors/have our needs met in legitimate ways. A vampire can rarely tell he/she is a vampire by looking in the mirror, he/she has to ask a friend, "Am I a vampire?"

Thanks—and thanks for sucking an hour away from my dissertation.

▼ ▼

My younger sister got married before I did. I was twenty-seven and still living at home. Bob was twenty-four and I thought he was gorgeous. Dark hair, great body, nice dresser. We danced together all the first night we met, and he bought all my drinks. What I remember most about that first meeting was that he was very, very smooth, especially for such a young guy. There was nothing awkward or unsure about him.

We started dating and he was wonderful, at least when we were together. He took me to the best clubs, always told me how beautiful I was, and gave me gifts. One of my friends told me that he was controlling, and that I was following the pattern of my family. For instance, he was always the one to call, and the few times I called him, he was definitely cool. When I told Bob what she said, joking, he got mad and made me stop seeing her. It was true that he wasn't interested in meeting my friends or attending any of my social functions. Later, I started seeing that he worked to pull me away from other people, especially people who weren't so charmed by him.

Even when we were dating, there would be periods when he would kind of disappear. Sometimes if I didn't hear from him for a few nights I would call even though I knew he didn't like it. Usually he wouldn't be home. If I brought it up or even left a message, he would explode, and convince me it was a sign that I didn't love or trust him.

After six months he finally asked me to marry him. What he didn't tell me was that he'd lost his job and was in a tight fix for money. I did notice that he let me pay for more and more of the things we did.

The next year was a flurry of parties, plans—it was what I always thought marriage should be. We felt like stars. Bob obviously liked the parties and the planning, but as the wedding got closer, he seemed to pull farther away. Sex changed, too; he seemed rougher and angrier. A few times I found him doing coke with friends, situations he had not invited me in on. It was another signal, like the money, that there were things going on he did not want me to know about. I did not dare ask; then he would really blow up.

After the wedding, things changed dramatically and quick. That was when I started to figure out that Bob was not really working. He would go out, but spend the day in a bar with his buddies, or watching a game somewhere. It got to be regular that he would stay out really late. At first we fought, then I got too tired of it, but then he would start a fight. The next day he would show up with flowers and take me out to dinner. And every few months he surprised me with plane tickets to the islands or Mexico—his mother was a travel agent. I always bragged to my friends about how romantic he was.

But it was getting to me, never knowing which way he was going to be, angry or romantic. I was worried, too, about our money, and the coke. Following my mother's advice, I opened my own bank account.

I became pregnant very soon after the wedding, and Bob was furious.

He started making mean comments about my body, calling me a "cow," and openly looking at other women. He lost interest in having sex with me. If I initiated it, or I guess if he was just horny, we might start, but I'd end up performing oral sex, and that would be it.

After our daughter was born he seemed pleased at first. Again, when I look back, I think what he enjoyed was the attention, the parties, plus the gifts we got from family. He was good at playing with the baby and good to me for the first few months. But then he started staying out late again. Now, with the baby to worry about, I started giving him ultimatums, and every time, a huge fight would occur. But it was always followed by another great week of making up, another trip to Florida. He would convince me, or I would convince myself, that he really wanted to work on our marriage.

For several more months, I left the baby with my mother and worked days. I cooked dinner every night, like a good wife. I did all the housework and laundry. Bob told me convincing stories about his work, and sometimes he brought home money.

Then one day I couldn't find my bank card. I assumed it had been stolen, and of course it was. By Bob. He had an explanation about grabbing it by mistake, thinking it was his. But 300 dollars turned up missing. This really scared me, not because of the money itself, but because it seemed like some kind of a step. But I was still really in love with him, and he was the father of my baby. I couldn't imagine life without him.

I got so desperate that one day I called in sick to work and followed him when he left the apartment. I sat in the car and watched as he pulled up to an attached brick house a few miles away and was met at the door by a pretty young blonde. There's no way to describe how I felt. I guess some part of me had suspected, but seeing it was unbelievable. I confronted him that night. He admitted that he had been seeing other women from the first. Not only would he not apologize, but he wasn't willing to stop. Not only that, but these women knew all about me and didn't care. Then I started to get what he was suggesting, that if I really loved him, I would go on supporting him while he slept around—that it was me who was disloyal and uncaring.

The next year was a nightmare. We separated. I stayed in the apartment with the baby. He moved back with his parents. He refused to give me money for child support until the court ordered it. He was incredibly vicious over the phone. Everyone was sick of the situation, my friends, parents, brothers, and sisters. They thought I was a fool. I knew I was a fool. Yet I could not seem to keep from calling him every night, to cry, beg, yell. When he wanted to, Bob would suddenly "make things right" for a little while— with a dinner, gift, even a smile. It kept me hoping.

I lost the weight I gained during pregnancy and then some. I was looking better, if you didn't count the dark circles. Bob started showing up early to visit our daughter, while she was still napping. He would be like he was in the old days, touching me, telling me I was beautiful, and I'd end up having sex with him. After he would leave, I literally felt like I had been drugged. There is no way to explain my behavior, why he had that power over me long after I knew what kind of man he was.

We have been divorced three years now, and I am still very vulnerable where he's concerned. I have to watch myself constantly. Every time I see him, it's like none of the awful stuff happened. I have to make a real effort to remember, to push back my feelings and stay remote. Sometimes I still weaken. The last time, he stopped by about four in the morning, after partying all night. I let him in. We had sex. He took a shower and left. I watched him out the window as he walked to his car, and it hit me how fresh and alert he looked.

I know a lot of women go through the same sort of thing with their husbands or boyfriends. I had never thought of it as anything like vampirism. That's exactly what it was. He sucked the life out of me for years, and in a way he still does. I ended up a wreck and he went sailing along.

I was sixteen when I met Matthew. I was a bad girl from a screwed-up family —he was the rich, good-looking son, seven years older. In the early years of living together we fought a lot and broke up a lot. I wanted to be an artist, but always supported myself in working-class jobs: waitress, forest service, glazing windows. Matthew said he wanted to break away from his investor father and society mother. We experimented, moving away from home, living in wild, remote places in the West.

After we married, however, we moved back to his hometown and Matthew went to work for his father. I became pregnant and then pregnant again and again. For five years my life was consumed with babies and houses. Matthew took great pleasure in molding me—buying me clothes, suggesting hair styles, picking furniture with me. At the time it didn't feel strange because I was still so young.

Once I emerged from my mothering fog, I began to notice eerie things about Matthew—things that I suppose had always been there, but I had been too in love to see. For instance, my reality did not correlate with Matthew's. I would hear him make arrangements with friends on the phone and later he would absolutely deny that he had said what I heard him say. He would give me an odd smile, clearly indicating that he thought I was the one who was crazy. I found out, accidentally, that he was having an affair with a young waitress in the city. Even though I had proof (phone bills, a photograph, letters) he denied that there was anything wrong with the relationship. He was just a friend to her.

He was constantly promising to support me in my art, or in any new business I might want to get involved in, and would then undercut me in subtle or not so subtle ways. He offered to pay for classes at the local university, but when I would get schedules and be at the point of signing up, there would be a problem with the time of the class, or he would ridicule my choice. As I began to spend more time on my art he complained that the house wasn't being kept the way he wanted it.

He would encourage me to take the kids up to our lake place in the summer, and then complain to friends about how spoiled I was, how out of touch with reality, how lucky I was to have the freedom to spend days at the lake while he had to work.

I began to notice that he went through friends more quickly than anyone else I knew. He would form intense friendships with other men, but after a short period of time they would explode in some bizarre disagreement. His version would always be very different from the other party's. He switched investment firms several times, always because the people at the firm were untrustworthy or dishonest.

I became aware that our financial situation was much weaker than he would ever admit. His parents, who had loaned us the money to buy our house, were, I believe, financing Matthew in other ways as well. He would never admit this to me, and would never let me in on the details of our financial situation. Then he would turn around and talk about how spoiled I was and how I didn't have any concept of how to budget our finances.

Once, when I was out of town, he went to see my best friend and talked to her for two hours about how all he wanted was for me to be happy, how he wanted to help me find myself, but that every time he offered help I would push him away or squander the opportunity. My friend said it was the most amazing performance she had ever seen. She had watched him sabotage me at every turn, completely sincere as he described for her my lack of discipline, my fuzzy nature, my inability to follow through on anything.

Sexually, things were unpleasant, but, again in a way that was very hard to pin down. It seemed he always wanted sex when I was most tired or at my weakest. Then he would run a hot bath for me and light candles. Instead of making me feel better, the sight of the candlelit bathroom would make my heart sink—I knew that this was his way of announcing that he *wanted sex. It began to feel like some kind of sacrificial ritual. If I resisted him I looked like the bad guy, after all the trouble he had gone to in setting a romantic mood. Often I just gave in; I never felt more lifeless than when he was on top of me.*

On business trips back to our hometown he started making a point of visiting our mutual friends, and even my friends and family, and telling them how "worried" he was about me. I was drinking too much, not getting out of bed till noon, neglecting the kids. God knows how long, how many people heard those things about me. I wasn't aware of what was going on until my sister heard the rumors from a casual acquaintance of hers and mine, and called me. Again, I felt like there was no way to defend myself. Matthew always spread the poison about me under the guise of his concern and love. If I denied the lies, I looked like I was in denial.

After a few years of what began to feel more and more like torture, I really had begun to fear going out of the house. I really did believe that I couldn't make a go of anything. In long, frequent talks with friends, family, and a therapist, I was constantly saying, "Look, here's what just happened. Am I crazy or is he?" Finally, I began to gather the strength to disengage from him and to begin divorce proceedings. When I reached that point, his total control seemed to crack for a while. He began to fly into rages, throwing things at me and shoving me. Once he nearly shoved me down a flight of stairs. After these attacks he would tell someone he was worried about my temper, or he was worried that I might hurt myself or others.

But once he realized that I was going to leave him, he quickly regained control, hiring a big-time lawyer, hiding whatever assets he had, holding an ugly custody fight over my head so I would agree to his financial terms. I felt lucky, at this point, to get out of the marriage alive. It was worth whatever it cost. Over eighteen years, I'd changed from a confident, risk-taking teenager to someone who was convinced that nothing I did was of any value or importance. For most of that time, I couldn't see any of it hap-

*pening. It was like I woke up one morning helpless, trapped, without a clue
as to how to change my situation. Then the really hard work began, getting
away from him and getting myself back.*

*It's been two years since the divorce and I am now regaining my strength
and self-confidence. Of course, we still have contact because of the kids, and
he can still make me feel totally crazy. The only defense is to keep these interactions as brief and as cold as possible.*

LOYALTY TESTS

As with sexual relationships, emotional vampirism in friendship can
take many forms. Here is a common one.

The tester (the emotional vampire) starts pressuring the testee
(victim) to share his dislike of a third person (enemy), usually a
friend or acquaintance to both, even though the enemy has personally done no wrong to the victim. In fact, the victim may in time
discover that the emotional vampire's complaints were exaggerated
or false.

This tends to be a lose-lose situation for the victim, right from
the start. If he yields, he's then on the outs with the enemy. If he
withstands, the emotional vampire will likely accuse him, tacitly or
explicitly, of taking the enemy's side; thus, that friendship will be
strained, and may even end.

The situation is then likely to turn on the victim, with the emotional vampire portraying him to other friends as an enemy:
untrustworthy, hurtful, in league with the powers of darkness (the
initial enemy). Turnaround is almost a given: the victim will be
blamed for the falling out between the emotional vampire and himself, which the emotional vampire has in fact forced. And so on.

Besides emotional consequences, the victim may suffer loss of friends and a damaged reputation. This is prime ground for the ripple effect, with distortion and exaggeration at every stage. Several or even many people may end up forced to take sides on others, whom they might hardly know.

Not uncommonly, the emotional vampire will eventually ally with his initial enemy, against the victim and/or others.

I have a very close friend, Constance. She's in her early forties, a scientist by training, mother of two young children whom she home schools. She's married to her childhood sweetheart. She's one of the most grounded and serious people I know. We talk for hours every week. Once, while on the phone with her, I started hearing something like a background rumble, and then it was eating up her life.

About two years ago, she discovered that her husband had been having an affair. They were in therapy, trying to mend their marriage, but she was on shaky ground, angry, hurt, questioning her life. To help cope, she immersed herself in learning about classical music.

Through her music connections, Constance met Linda, a composer, a very up-front lesbian, who dresses in a very butch way, black leather, jeans, all that. They didn't actually see each other at first, just talked on the phone about mutual interests, especially Mozart. When they did meet, Constance described it as overwhelmingly intense. Something about Linda overpowered her. They formed an immediate, highly emotional friendship. This surprised me, because Constance is tough, often very guarded with new people.

Linda was living with another woman, Trish. It was clear that Trish was emotionally troubled. She had been drummed out of the military, had attempted suicide in the recent past, and was unemployed. Linda was broke, too. She was always on the verge of signing with a major record company, or some other big development that never happened. One thing about the friendship became clear very quickly: if a meeting involved drinks or dinner, Constance paid. She also did a lot of chauffeuring, since Linda didn't drive. So it surprised me more when the two made plans to go to Europe together.

Constance had never been attracted to another woman or had any kind of lesbian affair, but pretty soon she was starting to think she was in love with Linda. They had nightly, hours-long phone calls. Linda worked both sides of the street. She talked about her love for Trish, and how much Trish needed her, but then would swear that she loved Constance and had never felt anything like this.

Linda treated Constance with clear ownership. Constance was not allowed to call her or initiate contact. But Linda demanded declarations of love and gave what amounted to commands about how Constance should live her life. Needless to say, this put a further strain on Constance's marriage and on her relationship with her kids. Early on, Linda took a very presumptive role with them, interfering with their lives and lecturing Constance on how to bring them up.

By now, Constance was tremendously confused about her feelings for Linda, and about her own sexuality. To complicate things further, she started spending time with Linda and Trish together. Pretty soon, Trish was deep in the act. She'd call Constance frequently, too, and spend a lot of time describing in intimate detail her sex life with Linda. Then, after this teasing, highly charged sex talk, Linda would call and be very authoritative, acting as if she owned Constance.

Both women started spending a lot of time at Constance's home, intruding into the life of her kids. They dismissed her husband outright and insisted she was really gay. He was very uncomfortable around them—used the word "creepy"—but he felt very badly about his affair and was genuinely trying to get the marriage back on track. It seemed clear that Linda and Trish knew this and used it—just like they knew they had come upon her at a particularly vulnerable time.

A *bizarre triangle developed. The three women would sit up late laying out Tarot cards for each other. Trish or Linda would leave the room and the other one would confide in Constance, expressing their jealousy or love. Frequently, Trish would throw a tantrum or threaten to hurt herself, and Linda would cut off contact with Constance. But this never lasted long. She'd call when Trish was out, and then Trish would call, tearfully begging forgiveness. Constance and Linda went for a drive and spent hours parked, kissing like teenagers—and then Linda suddenly cut off all contact because Trish threatened to kill herself.*

Constance felt totally consumed. Her husband spent most of his time in his shop by now, and she knew her kids' schooling was suffering but she felt powerless to change it.

I had heard about all this several times a week for months. Then Constance and her kids came to visit me for ten days. Linda and Trish started calling my house the minute she arrived, and both started flirting with me (I'm female, divorced, hetero). Their seductiveness was undeniable.

Constance by now was considering leaving her husband and forming a relationship with these women. They had not so subtly started pressuring her to loan them money.

Then Trish decided on a new career move—apprenticing herself to a dominatrix. Constance finally seemed to take a look at the effect this all was having on her kids. She suspected, rightly, that it wasn't over, but she went to Europe by herself. She'd gotten very into Mozart, toured Vienna and Prague, and everything she saw reminded her of Linda.

This is the strangest part of all this. On the plane home, she sat next to an elderly woman, a stranger, who said, "My God, what has happened to you?"

Constance answered in very vague terms: she'd been on an emotional trip, visiting sites connected with Mozart, and that kept reminding her of a very strong bond with someone.

Her seat mate then spoke to her very kindly, but firmly, telling her that important as this connection was, it was draining her, and she had to cut it. The elderly woman then described the process to do this. When Constance got home, she had to cast a spell. She should visualize the parts of her body that she associated with Linda's presence, the points where the presence entered into her.

She should then mix up different paints, gold and silver among them, and paint patterns on her body which would protect her. She was also supposed to say certain things, and visualize the painted markings as a strong protective barrier against the presence.

Constance did it, soon after her return home. Linda called, and they went out to dinner, but she felt an immediate change in how she reacted. She still loved Linda, but no longer felt powerless to resist her demands. She was her old, tough self again.

Both Linda and Trish called again, wanting, of all things, to organize a birthday party for one of Constance's sons. Constance put them off. Soon another crisis came up, Trish moving out on Linda. The door was open—it seemed—for Constance and Linda to get together. Constance held firm, and Trish came back.

Now the phone calls have trickled to a couple a year. Constance talks about the whole episode as if she was temporarily insane. She feels free of both of them. But she's amazingly uncritical, especially of Linda. It about put her under, but I think it was the most passionate experience of her life.

VAMPIRIC PATRONAGE

A well-known and frequently dramatized scenario involves an individual with power—whether as money, influence, the ability to advance a career, or some other form—who links up with a protégé, usually younger, and essentially trades the material favors for emotional energy, in the form of attention, sex, etc.—and likely, submission. This can also go the other way, with the protégé being the emotional vampire, and draining the older patron.

In their nature, such relationships tend to be more vampiric than most, with both parties aware that they're using and being used. Still, the consequences can be grim, particularly if the emotional vampire is unscrupulous, and the victim, naive. Once he's no longer of use, he may be discarded.

It's also a likely situation in which to encounter actually dangerous emotional vampires.

CULTS AND MASS VAMPIRISM

Cults are another serious and complex phenomenon, far too broad for us to do more than touch on. We will only note that in some striking instances, a form of group emotional vampirism seems indicated.

This usually involves a charismatic figure surrounding himself with acolytes who fall increasingly under his power. Usually, there's a higher ideal—a spiritual entity, or a cause—which he claims to represent personally. The acolytes' energy, which is devoted to that ideal—one that can be extremely profound and personal, especially if religious—in fact gets largely channeled to the predator, who then uses it, and his followers, to continually enhance his position.

It can be difficult to distinguish between a leader's self-centered aims and genuine religious or political fervor. As with personal relationships, the two things are likely to be blurred. Also, such leaders often start out sincere and become corrupted. They may themselves lose the ability to distinguish.

Such figures, together with their immediate circle of disciples, may enjoy extraordinary energy that takes many forms, including enhanced personal vitality, while those farther at the fringes diminish. Followers are likely to be drained of individual will in a way that's often compared to brainwashing. Groups may tend toward a single mass personality, bland, devoid of real thought, reflecting only what the leader allows (including adulation of him). Individuals may be strong and energetic in the context of the cult, but separated, they may be aimless, lethargic, even suicidal.

Like certain other forms of emotional vampirism, a "guru" in the presence of a group of his disciples can be an eerie thing to watch.

Other types of groups, from gangs to large-scale political movements, can exhibit similar effects. History gives numerous examples, sometimes entailing vast, real destruction—wars, crusades, and general chaos. Recent decades add other notable examples, like Jonestown.

We'll also mention here other impersonal and/or mass phenomena which can be regarded as vampiric: militaristic regimes which brutalize and starve their people so that an elite can enjoy wealth and power; corporations which destroy the livelihoods of large numbers of domestic workers by sending their jobs to third-world countries, where workers labor for subsistence wages under unsafe and environmentally hazardous conditions; rampant consumerism, no-brain television, and the like, which leech away time and energy, especially from young people, which most would agree could better be spent on other pursuits.

Mutual Vampirism

Finally, there is an up side to all this. Whether conscious energy sharing among consenting adults can really be called vampirism remains a question. But during the writing of this book, it came increasingly to our attention that many people practice this, both privately and in groups. It can have its own rules and etiquette, and brings to mind the human batteries we've mentioned.

Emotional vampires . . . never heard them called that . . . always thought it was called Psychic Vampirism (oh well . . . everything else has many names, too). Know a lot of them. I know how to be one. I have "fed" off the energy of others when it was needed (although I usually take the energy that comes off a group instead of energy from one person, unless I know the person and have their permission). It is not always a bad experience. I will willingly give up the energy I get from my friends when they need it. I know you weren't trying to offend in your post, I just am afraid that people are going to get the wrong idea from your book (no offense meant at all).

7

A Look at Dracula

Ah, it is the fault of our science that wants to explain all; and if
it explain not, then it says there is nothing to explain. But yet we
see around us every day the growth of new beliefs, which think
themselves new; and which are yet but the old, which pretend to be
young—like the fine ladies at the opera.

Bram Stoker, Dracula (1897)

At the heart of the vampire fascination rampant in today's
society lies the story of *Dracula*—now celebrating its one hun-
dredth anniversary of publication—which has engendered a veri-
table industry, with a wealth of film, fiction, spin-offs, pop culture,
and serious historical research.

The classic vampire figure as it evolved into Count Dracula—

gaunt, sinister, and yet outwardly human; even possessed of an eccentric elegance; and above all, powerful—was recognizable before the novel *Dracula* came along. No less a luminary than Lord Byron had created such a character, as did several other nineteenth-century writers. These in turn were built on legends of (supposedly) actual bloodsucking corpses, which were especially prevalent in the Balkans and Eastern Europe.

It was Bram Stoker's genius to link all that with a historical reality, one of the grimmest on record.

Dracula's home of Transylvania—in the Carpathian Mountains, now part of Romania—was almost as remote as the moon, and probably as mysterious, to the average Englishman of one hundred years ago. The history of the region and its surroundings is a particularly bloody one. It has been an uneasy melting pot for millennia, with many different peoples coming into close and often violent contact. Political, religious, and ethnic warfare has been constant since prefeudal times. Among other factors, its location, in the pathway between harsh lands to the north and east, and the richer, warmer country of the Black Sea and Mediterranean, made it prone to invasion: Goths and Vikings from the north; successive waves of Huns, Magyars, and Mongols from central Asia; and, during the later Middle Ages, Turks seeking to move westward into Europe, all creating a battleground of endless attacks and retreats. This legacy has continued with the major conflicts of this century.

The figure that Stoker chose as the quintessential vampire sprang from this breeding ground. He was a powerful Romanian noble of the fifteenth century, with the given name of Vlad. Dracul or Dracula was a clan name, stemming from "dragon," with the connotation of "devil." His violent life has been well chronicled, most notably in Raymond T. McNally and Radu Florescu's *In Search of Dracula.*

Suffice it to say here that he is known to history as Vlad the Impaler. In the long campaign he waged against invading Turks, a war which stood out for its savagery even in those times, he did not hesitate to impale thousands, including his own subjects, as a warning to the enemy.

"The evil that men do lives after them," Shakespeare wrote. Ancient, and not so ancient, history gives us plenty of figures who are remembered mainly for their brutality.

But in his novel, Bram Stoker goes out of his way to add extra dimensions to his villain. Early on, speaking to Jonathan Harker about a warrior ancestor (who, of course, is really the Count himself), Dracula refers to a disastrous battle which he fled, leaving his army to be butchered. But he makes it clear that he did this not out of cowardice: rather, because he believed that he was the only man alive who could regroup his people and ultimately win the war.*

Stoker's intention seems to be to portray a man who, terrible though he was, stood out for qualities remarkable in his era. Among medieval barons, personal honor was at the highest premium. There are many stories of men riding into certain slaughter, essentially so

---

*In fact, the incident to which Stoker is probably referring, a campaign on the Danube in 1461, was not so clearcut. Vlad did retreat, and ended up fleeing for his life, although the record does not suggest any such high-minded motive. What was left of his army seems to have abandoned him, rather than the other way around. But there is no doubt that he was a steel-nerved warrior. History credits him with a major role in stopping the Turks' advance. Nikolae Ceausescu, Romania's recent ghoulish dictator, made an effort to turn Vlad into a national hero, even issuing a commemorative postage stamp.

they would not be called cowards, and rare indeed was the noble who took a longer view than what he could gain at the point of his own sword. Fiefdoms, kingdoms, and thousands of lives, especially those of the common people, were tossed around like gambling chips.

Instead, we are presented with Vlad's iron determination to win the long fight and save his nation, even at the sacrifice of his own honor, with an utter contempt for what his peers might think.

This and other touches combine in the novel to make the Count far more complex than a bloodthirsty fiend. There is something of the tragic figure in him: overstated, melodramatized, supernatural-ized, but eerily human.

Initially, he plays the nobly gracious host to Harker. He's a fas-cinating companion, with vast knowledge and intelligence. He speaks with stirring pride of his family's warrior heritage, and refers pointedly to the blood of Attila himself, flowing in his veins. As the story develops, his courage in action and his will in carrying out his plans are ferocious. He is evil, but there is nothing small or spine-less about him: he is the most formidable of adversaries.

Perhaps most striking of all, we learn that he has loved. The story resolves into his obsession with Mina Harker. He intends to make her his eternal companion; and to seal their bond, he forces, or allows, her to drink from his own veins. Thus, we are introduced to the archetypal struggle between Evil and the powers of Good (represented by the several men, especially Van Helsing) for an innocent soul.

Much as we loathe and fear Dracula, we see glimmers of our-selves in him: empathizing with his passion, admiring his intelli-gence and strength, perhaps even pitying him.

This tension between Dracula as demonic and Dracula as

human infuses the novel. We are continually reminded of it, as the Count masterfully manipulates the emotions of his enemies, confusing and seducing them. The psychological effects suffered by his victims and those around them are described in strikingly similar terms to emotional vampirism. In fact, a close reading yields many passages that reinforce points we have touched on in this book, and illuminate related aspects.

The authors suspect that this link has much to do with the novel's undying popularity. It brings the bloodsucking vampire of legend into the realm of everyday reality. He is not a threat separate and apart, descending only to destroy, and always remaining *other.* In the common currency of human feeling—emotion—he is like us.

What follows is a look at *Dracula* as a paradigm for emotional vampirism: the foggy, undiscovered country where man and monster meet.

To explore this, we have excerpted a number of quotes from the novel and divided them into major groups:

- NATURE: comments that underline major aspects of emotional vampirism;
- SYMPTOMS: signs that a victim has been attacked;
- ANTIDOTES: means of self-defense and healing.

These quotes refer mainly to the more serious forms of emotional vampirism, in keeping with the Count's status as the most actually dangerous of all.

NATURE

"Welcome to my house! Enter freely and of your own will . . . and leave something of the happiness you bring!"

Count Dracula invites Harker into the castle, suggesting, with grim humor, that he'll be bled of his "happiness." The emphasis on free will foreshadows the importance of seduction, rather than force. Dracula craves the submission of his chosen victim, Mina: not just her body, but her soul.

"The light and warmth and the Count's courteous welcome seemed to dissipate all my doubts and fears."

The seduction begins with attention, comfort, and charm.

"The Count saw his victory in my bow, and his mastery in the trouble of my face, for he began at once to use them, but in his own smooth, resistless way. . . ."

Dracula manipulates Harker into staying at the castle, lengthening the interaction.

"How dare you touch him, any of you? How dare you cast eyes on him when I had forbidden it? Back, I tell you all! This man belongs to me!"

The vampire brides try to "kiss" Harker. Emotional vampires don't like to share victims.

"Be careful with him always that there may be nothing to excite him of this kind for a long time to come; the traces of such an illness as his do not lightly die away."

Sister Agatha writing Mina regarding Harker's illness. The

effects may be serious and long-lasting, and a recovering victim may remain susceptible to the emotional vampire.

" 'Look!' he cried suddenly. 'There's something in the wind and in the hoast beyont that sounds, and looks, and tastes, and smells like death. It's in the air and comin'.' "

Mina's conversation with a local fisherman, as the storm blows Dracula's ship in. A level of perception deeper than education or sophistication may warn of the emotional vampire's approach.

"Every spar, rope, and stay was strained, and some of the 'top-hammer' came crashing down. But strangest of all, the very instant the shore was touched, an immense dog sprang up on deck from below, as if shot up by the concussion, and running forward, jumped from the bow on the sand. . . ."

The wrecked ship washes up at Whitby, its crew dead to a man: except for Dracula. Beware the person who steps from chaos unscathed, leaving carnage and misery behind.

"The bride-maidens rejoice the eyes that wait the coming of the bride; but when the bride draweth nigh, then the maidens shine not to the eyes that are filled."

Renfield. When a fresher, more attractive victim comes along, the previous one is likely to be discarded, or reduced to the role of minor sycophant.

"In all these cases the children were too young to give any properly intelligible account, but the consensus of their excuses is that they had been with a 'bloofer lady.' "

Lucy begins her vampiric career, starting, like many emotional vampires, with the weakest victims.

"She lay in her Vampire sleep, so full of life and voluptuous beauty that I shudder as though I have come to do murder. Ah, I have no doubt that in old time, when such things were, many a man who set forth to do such a task as mine, found at the last his heart fail him, and then his nerve. So he delay, and delay, and delay, till the mere beauty and the fascination of the wanton Un-Dead have hypnotise him; and he remain on and on, till sunset come, and the Vampire sleep be over. Then the beautiful eyes of the fair woman open and look love, and the voluptuous mouth present to a kiss—and man is weak. And there remain one more victim in the Vampire fold. . . ."

Van Helsing. The emotional vampire's charm, seductiveness, and promise of giving the victim what he wants are extremely difficult to overcome.

"I am so worried in my mind that I am apt to be irritable. If only you knew the problem I have to face, and what I am working out, you would pity, and tolerate, and pardon me. Pray do not put me in a straight-coat. I want to think and I cannot think freely when my body is confined."

Renfield. Dracula's mind-clouding and emotional torment of him are leapfrogging off each other. There's also a recognizable attempt at turnaround.

"All day I waited to hear from him, but he did not send me anything, not even a blow-fly, and when the moon got up I was pretty angry with him. When he slid in through the window, though it was shut, and did not even knock, I was mad with him. He sneered at me, and his white face looked out of the mist with his red eyes gleaming, and he went on as though he owned the whole place, and I was no one."

Renfield is no longer useful to the vampire: he has been drained, and Dracula is on to choicer game.

"He meant escape. Hear me, ESCAPE! He saw that with but one earth-box left, and a pack of men following like dogs after a fox, this London was no place for him. He take his last earth-box on board a ship, and he leave the land."

Van Helsing. The emotional vampire puts his own well-being above all. He won't hesitate to abandon a victim who might have come to depend on him.

"I *know* that [Mina] forms conclusions of her own, and from all that has been I can guess how brilliant and how true they must be; but she will not, or cannot, give them utterance. . . . The Count had his own purposes when he gave her what Van Helsing called 'the Vampire's baptism of blood.' "

Seward, after Mina has drunk from Dracula's veins. If the victim yields significantly to the emotional vampire's seduction, he may withdraw from others and keep the depth of the interaction secret.

"The criminal always work at one crime—that is the true criminal who seems predestinate to crime, and who will of none other."

Van Helsing. The emotional vampire will tend to choose similar victims, and operate in similar ways.

"His past is a clue, and the one page of it we know—and that from his own lips—tells that once before, when in what Mr. Morris would call a 'tight place,' he went back to his own country from the land he had tried to invade, and thence, without losing purpose, prepared himself for a new effort."

Mina Harker. An emotional vampire who has already hit a victim once may make a friendly return, looking for a safe situation—possibly because he is on the run from another that has fallen through.

"Everything had been carefully thought out, and done systematically and with precision. He seemed to have been prepared for every obstacle which might be placed by accident in the any of his intentions being carried out. . . . I saw the invoice, and took note of it: 'Fifty cases of common earth, to be used for experimental purposes.' "

Harker, describing Dracula's preparations for moving to England. The emotional vampire will lay groundwork carefully, and will have a logical, innocent explanation for odd occurrences.

"It is said, too, that he can only pass running water at the slack or the flood of the tide."

Van Helsing. An addendum to the bridge/running water myth: the emotional vampire's attack will be most successful when the victim's emotional energy, and defenses, are low; he'll feed best when the energy is running strong.

"For it is not the least of its terrors that this evil thing is rooted deep in all good; in soil barren of holy memories it cannot rest."

Van Helsing. The emotional vampire can only thrive among "good," emotionally rich victims.

"But the room was awfully stuffy. There were a lot of those horrible, strong-smelling flowers about everywhere, and she actually had a bunch of them around her neck. I feared that the heavy odour would be too much for the dear child in her weak state, so I took them all away and opened a bit of the window to let in a little fresh air."

Lucy's mother, as unwitting enabler. Those who don't understand what the victim is going through, however good their intentions, may add to the trouble through lack of sympathy, or even facilitate the vampire's assaults.

"Strange that it never struck me that the very next house might be the Count's hiding-place!"

Mina. Emotional vampires tend to be so close as to escape notice, often remaining unrecognized for long periods.

"They are *very, very* suspicious."

Mina, regarding the people of Transylvania, and their centuries of experience with vampires. Rational skepticism is well and good, but looking deeper might save your neck.

SYMPTOMS

"If I be sane, then surely it is maddening to think that of all the foul things that lurk in this hateful place the Count is the least dreadful to me; that to him alone I can look for safety, even though this be only whilst I can serve his purpose."

Harker, in Castle Dracula. The victim may look to the emotional vampire for harbor and comfort, when the latter is the one who has caused the trouble to begin with.

"I passed to my room and went to bed, and, strange to say, slept without dreaming. Despair has its own charms."

Harker, after encountering the castle's deepest horrors. The victim may experience a state of lethargy, his life reduced to meeting simple needs.

"Another week gone, and no news from Jonathan, not even to Mr. Hawkins, from whom I have heard. Oh, I do hope he is not ill. He surely would have written. I look at that last letter of his, but somehow it does not satisfy me. It does not read like him, and yet it is his writing."

Mina, while Harker is still in Transylvania. The victim's friends and family may note that he's not his old self, and even cease seeing and hearing from him.

". . . she will not admit to me that there is any cause for restlessness; or if there be, she does not understand it herself."

Mina, speaking of Lucy's sleepwalking. The victim may resist attempts to bring him out of his state.

"Oh, but I am tired! If it were not that I had made my diary a duty I should not open it tonight."

Mina, nursing her husband, before her own attack. The ripple effect among the victim's friends and family, with their energy being sapped in turn.

". . . even at such a time, when her body must have been chilled with cold, and her mind somewhat appalled at waking unclad in a churchyard at night, she did not lose her grace."

Mina, after Lucy has sleepwalked to be bled by Dracula. The

victim may cease to care about, or be embarrassed by, anything else, including his own bizarre behavior.

"The adventure of the night does not seem to have harmed her; on the contrary, it has benefitted her, for she looks better this morning than she has done for weeks."

Mina, the following day. After an emotional crisis, such as the shock of realizing he has been used, the victim may feel better, and temporarily come to his senses. This may include the "that was the last time, I swear" syndrome.

". . . twice during the night I was wakened by Lucy trying to get out. She seemed, even in her sleep, to be a little impatient at finding the door shut, and went back to bed under a sort of protest."

Mina. Chances are the relief won't last long.

"I don't want to talk to you; you don't count now; the Master is at hand."

Renfield. The emotional vampire may displace everyone else in the victim's affections.

"I have had a great shock, and when I try to think of what it is I feel my head spin round, and I do not know if it was all real or the dreaming of a madman."

Harker to Mina, in Budapest. Afterward, the victim may think he has actually been insane.

"With you I agree that there has been much blood lost; it has been, but is not. But the conditions of her are in no way anemic."

Van Helsing's medical assessment of Lucy. The victim's condition is not attributable to normally identifiable causes.

"All this weakness comes to me in sleep; until I dread the very thought."

Lucy's diary. On a deep level, the victim knows what's happening, and self-preservation instincts will struggle with the drive to yield.

". . . the draining away of one's blood, no matter how willingly it be given, is a terrible feeling."

Seward, on donating blood to Lucy. Those not under the emotional vampire's spell are appalled by the victim's loss of vitality—and the draining they themselves may experience secondarily.

"I have a dim half-remembrance of long, anxious times of waiting and fearing; darkness in which there was not even the pain of hope to make present distress more poignant: and then long spells of oblivion, and the rising back to life as a diver coming up through a great press of water."

Lucy, describing her enthrallment.

"He says the amount of responsibility which it puts on him makes him nervous. He begins to doubt himself. I try to cheer him up, and *my* belief in *him* helps him to have a belief in himself. But it is here that the grave shock that he experienced tells upon him the most. Oh, it is too hard that a sweet, simple, noble, strong nature such as his . . . should be so injured that the very essence of its strength is gone."

Mina, speaking of Harker. More real consequences of the vampire's assault: he is beginning to fail at his profession.

"Dr. Van Helsing, what I have to tell you is so queer that you must not laugh at me or at my husband. I have been since yesterday in a sort of fever of doubt; you must be kind to me, and not think me foolish that I have even half believed some very strange things."

Mina. The idea of an emotional vampire attack may sound unbelievable to most.

"When Lucy—I call the thing that was before us Lucy because it bore her shape—saw us she drew back with an angry snarl . . . with a careless motion, she flung to the ground, callous as a devil, the child that up to now she had clutched strenuously to her breast, growling over it as a dog growls over a bone."

Seward, as the men prepare to destroy Lucy. However smooth the cover, the emotional vampire's true nature will show if he's exposed, as by the sunlight of recognition.

" 'Come to me, Arthur. Leave these others and come to me. My arms are hungry for you. Come, and we can rest together. Come, my husband, come!'

"There was something diabolically sweet in her tones—something of the tinkling of glass when struck—which rang through the brains even of us who heard the words addressed to another. As for Arthur, he seemed under a spell. . . ."

Seward. The emotional vampire will promise exactly what the victim wants. The victim—especially if recovering—may know it's a lie, but go for it anyway.

"I could not for my life get away from the feeling that there was some one else amongst us. . . . I think the feeling was common to us all. . . ."

Harker. A powerful vampire may obsess the victim, with a constant fascination which may include love—and dread.

"Everything that one does seems, no matter how right it may be, to bring on the very thing, which is most to be deplored. If I hadn't gone to Whitby, perhaps poor dear Lucy would be with us now. She hadn't taken to visiting the churchyard till I came, and if she hadn't come there in the day-time with me she wouldn't have walked there in her sleep; and if she hadn't gone there at night and asleep, that monster couldn't have destroyed her as he did. . . . There now, crying again! I, who never cried in my life. . . ."

The ripple effect becomes concentrated in Mina, setting her up as the next victim. Irrational guilt over Lucy is weakening her. The assault has already begun.

". . . the cloudy column was now whirling in the room, and through it all came the scriptural words 'a pillar of cloud by day and of fire by night.' Was it indeed some such spiritual guidance that was coming to me in my sleep?"

Mina, recounting her first, unknown, meeting with Dracula. The emotional vampire's seduction takes many forms, and the victim may go out of his way to see it as a romantic, even sacred, one.

" 'So, so!' I thought to myself, 'this is the second time he has suddenly stopped at the word "drink"; what does it mean?' "

Seward, speaking of Renfield, with a Freudian touch. Both emotional vampire and victim may reveal themselves through unintentional words and actions.

". . . the . . . the . . . the . . . Vampire. (Why did I hesitate to write the word?)"

Mina, in an echo of the above. This time, the sense is of denial.

"Then, ere the great dark came upon is—for even after sundown the heavens reflected the gone sun upon the snow, and all was for a time in a great twilight. . . . I make a fire; and near it I make Madam Mina, now awake and more charming than ever, sit comfortable among her rugs."

Van Helsing, in a letter to Seward. The victim will begin to perk up when the vampire is near, or can be expected (sundown).

"I suppose it is thus that in old times one vampire meant many; just as their hideous bodies could only rest in sacred earth, so the holiest love was the recruiting sergeant for their ghastly ranks . . . for that faith it would be easier to die than to live, and so be quit of all the trouble."

Harker despairs at watching his wife destroyed—and recognizes that vampirism preys particularly on love and generosity.

ANTIDOTES

"It is for others' good that I ask—to redress great wrong, and to lift much and terrible troubles. . . ."

Van Helsing, to Mina. Exposing the emotional vampire is a service to future victims.

(Van Helsing personifies defense against vampirism. He is no superhero; his fear of Dracula is evident, and he makes serious mistakes, almost costing Mina her soul. But he is clear-sighted, dedi-

cated, compassionate, and humble. He's also effective, largely because—like his archenemy—he's unconcerned about the opinions of
his peers. Their battle is with each other, in an arena that's off the
maps.)

". . . I must somehow learn the facts of his journey abroad. The time
is come, I fear, when I must open that parcel, and know what is
written. Oh, Jonathan, you will, I know, forgive me if I do wrong,
but it is for your own dear sake."

Mina, on her husband's continued disturbance. To make sense of
the victim's behavior, friends and family have to become aware of
the emotional vampire.

"I shall try to save him from it; but it may be even a consolation and
a help to him—terrible though it be and awful in its consequences—to know for certain this eyes and ears and brain did not
deceive him, and that it was all true."

Mina, speaking of Harker. Afterward, the victim may doubt
whether he can say with truth that his trouble did stem from emotional vampirism, and even doubt his sanity. The understanding
and experiences of others can help confirm it.

"You tell not your madmen what you do nor why you do it; you tell
them not what you think. So you shall keep knowledge in its place,
where it may rest—where it may gather its kind around it and
breed."

Van Helsing. In countering the emotional vampire, it's often
prudent to act indirectly and subtly, and play one's cards close to
one's chest.

"There is no time to be lost. She will die for sheer want of blood to keep the heart action as it should be. There must be transfusion of blood at once. Is it you or me?"

Van Helsing, speaking of Lucy. More ripple effect. The victim may require charges of energy from friends and family, especially in crises.

"He must then go home and rest, sleep and eat much, that he may be recruited of what he has given to his love."

Van Helsing, after Holmwood has given his blood to Lucy. The victim's friends won't be able to help if they, too, allow themselves to be sucked in.

"First he fastened up the windows and latched them securely; next, taking a handful of the flowers, he rubbed them all over the sashes, as though to ensure that every whiff of air that might get in would be laden with the garlic smell. Then with the wisp he rubbed all over the jamb of the door, above, below, and at each side, and round the fireplace in the same way. . . ."

Van Helsing's precautions: extreme watchfulness and a psychologically guarded environment, allowing the emotional vampire no point of entrance.

". . . there are things that you know not, but that you shall know, and bless me for knowing, though they are not pleasant things."

Van Helsing, warning against the false compassion of refusing to recognize vampiric predations.

"Ah, we men and women are like ropes drawn tight with strain that pull us different ways. . . . But King Laugh he come like the sunshine, and he ease off the strain again; and we bear to go on with our labour, what it may be."

Van Helsing, after Lucy's funeral. Humor won't stop the emotional vampire, but it may help both victim and others close.

"I am so glad he has plenty of work to do, for that keeps his mind off the terrible things. . . ."

Mina, speaking of her husband. Apathy for work and other healthy aspects of life is a notable, and costly, consequence of the predation. Restoring them—even if, at first, against the victim's will—can be powerful therapy.

"She showed me in the doctor's letter that all wrote down was true. It seems to have made a new man of me. It was the doubt as to the reality of the whole thing that knocked me over. I felt impotent, and in the dark, and distrustful. But now that I *know,* I am not afraid, even of the Count."

Harker: the power of recognition and acceptance.

". . . there are things done to-day in electrical science which would have been deemed unholy by the very men who discovered electricity—who would themselves not so long before have been burned as wizards."

Van Helsing, on keeping a genuinely open mind.

"He [Arthur, Lucy's fiancé] must have one hour that will make the very face of heaven grow black to him; then we can act for good all round send him peace."

Van Helsing, on his decision to demonstrate Lucy in the act of vampirism. Victims and those close to them will resist the idea of an emotional vampire at work unless cause and effect are pointed out clearly.

". . . for all that die from the preying of the Un-Dead become themselves Un-Dead, and prey on their kind. And so the circle goes on ever widening, like the ripples from a stone thrown in the water. . . . The career of this so unhappy dear lady is but just begun. Those children whose blood she suck are not as yet so much the worse, but if she live on, Un-Dead, more and more they lose their blood and by her power over them, they come to her; and so she draw their blood with that so wicked mouth. But if she die in truth, then all cease; the tiny wounds of the throats disappear. . . ."

Van Helsing. The ripple effect will continue unless the emotional vampire is neutralized.

"The stake must be driven through her. It will be a fearful ordeal— be not deceived in that—but it will be only a short time, and you will then rejoice more than your pain was great; from this grim tomb you will emerge as though you tread on air."

Van Helsing. The victim will only find real peace by coming to terms with the emotional vampire and severing the tie. This requires great strength.

"That going down to the vault a second time was a remarkable piece of daring. After reading his account of it I was prepared to meet a good specimen of manhood, but hardly the quiet, business-like gentleman who came here to-day."

Seward, speaking of Harker. Unflashy, steady fortitude is a central quality of effectively dealing with emotional vampirism.

"Mrs. Harker gave us a cup of tea, and I can honestly say that, for the first time since I have lived in it, this old house seemed like *home.*"

Seward. The victim (Mina) is still in danger, but the vampire has been identified and the friends have sworn to give battle: the first important steps in healing. The house is a primary Freudian image for the body.

"We have on our side power of combination—a power denied to the vampire kind; we have sources of science; we are free to act and think; and the hours of the day and night are ours equally. In fact, so far as our powers extend, they are unfettered, and we are free to use them. . . . He can do all these things, yet he is not free. . . . His power ceases, as does that of all evil things, at the coming of the day."

Van Helsing. The emotional vampire's tactics are limited, and his greatest strength in attack—his own selfish need—is in the long run his great weakness: he can't thrive without the victim. The victim's primary strength lies in clear understanding; from there, he can find options for defense or withdrawal.

". . . the brute beasts which are to the Count's command are yet themselves not amenable to his spiritual power; for look, these rats that would come to his call . . . run pell-mell from the so little dogs of my friend Arthur."

Van Helsing. In combination, together with mind-clouding, the emotional vampire's tactics are powerful. Taken individually, they're much easier to counter.

" '. . . you are to be punished for what you have done. You have aided in thwarting me; now you shall come to my call. When my brain says "Come!" to you, you shall cross land or sea to do my bidding; and to that end this!' With that he pulled open his shirt, and with his long sharp nails opened a vein in his breast. When the blood began to spurt out, he took my hands in one of his, holding them tight, and with the other seized my neck and pressed my mouth to the wound. . . ."

Mina's first physical encounter with Dracula. A graphic depiction of successful seduction, with mutual need arising in the victim.

"No, you must live! You must struggle and strive to live, though death would seem a book unspeakable. You must fight Death himself. . . ."

Van Helsing, forbidding Mina's suicide plans. The victim must shake off despair and lethargy, and arouse the determination to save himself.

"He think, too, that as he cuts himself off from knowing your mind, there can be no knowledge of him to you. . . ."

Van Helsing, on Mina's mind-meld with Dracula. Another weakness of the emotional vampire's narrow-mindedness, and an odd psychological quirk, perhaps related to intense egotism. He's likely to enter new situations with similar tactics, not realizing that the insights of former victims can be used against him in future.

"I shall be glad as long as I live that even in that moment of final dissolution, there was in his face a look of peace, such as I could never have imagined might have rested there before."

Mina, on Dracula's demise. A complex of emotions is suggested, which comprise a good summary from a recovered victim: the generous spirit that made her a prime victim, with her pitying him and wishing him well, even after he nearly destroyed her; the bond of intense shared emotion, exciting and powerful in spite of it all—and her deep attraction to him, beneath her hatred.

Appendix

Emotional Vampirism in Drama: A Very Brief Survey

A s we've noted, the supernatural vampire is widely celebrated in literature and film. So is his energy-draining counterpart, although he's not as readily recognized.

A closer look reveals that many of our greatest dramas involve, and are often based on, intensely vampiric relationships. The surface-level stakes may be more graphic: wealth, power, murder. But it's the emotional tension between the players that gives these stories their deeper force. Looking at them from the perspective of emotional vampirism is an excellent way to broaden the perspective of what we've described, in terms of widespread human experience through different times and places.

The list that follows includes mostly classics, with a few less mainstream examples to illuminate different perspectives. Many have

191

been presented as fiction, film, and/or drama, sometimes in several different versions. We're identifying them by their original titles.

Our comments, like the list itself, are far short of comprehensive; like most of this book, this section is intended to point to a way of seeing.

The film *All About Eve* exemplifies a common theme in line with what we've described as vampiric patronage: in the world of art or society, an established, powerful figure gets involved with a protégé/would-be. This turns to struggle, until one or the other is consumed. There are many variations and complications, including other phenomena we've touched on, such as ripple effect. The relationships are often sexual. Other classic examples include: *The Blue Angel, The Red Shoes, A Star Is Born, Sunset Boulevard.*

A similar scenario—of a self-centered character draining and discarding others—is at least as common, and occurs in a wider context. It may be oblique, subordinate (but integral) to the main story (*Cabaret, The Hustler, La Strada, To Die For*).

Anna Karenina is driven into despair and suicide by a combination of forces, but key among them is her husband's refusal to grant her a divorce. This, in turn, is carefully engineered by the bloodless Countess Lydia Ivanovna, under the guise of piousness. In fact, she's keenly intent on devastating Anna.

Cat on a Hot Tin Roof, The Glass Menagerie, A Streetcar Named Desire, and most of Tennessee Williams's other works are heavily based on the characters' predatory emotional interactions. Less well known is his short story "Desire and the Black Masseur." It's extremely interesting, both about vampirism and the author.

Chinatown reveals the triumphant evil of Noah Cross, on both macro- and microcosmic levels: he destroys an entire valley by draining its water, and destroys his daughters' lives through incest.

Doctor Faustus, in its several versions, is the great dramatization of the Devil's Bargain. In Thomas Mann's novel, the composer Leverkuhn deliberately contracts syphilis to acquire—temporary—brilliance. The tragic consequences are played out vampirically, in his relationship with his nephew Nepomuk.

Doctor Jekyll and Mister Hyde can be seen as another great metaphor, of a man yielding to the vampire within himself.

Fatal Attraction created a stir equaled by few films. In it, Glenn Close consumes the lives, first of Michael Douglas, then of his family—and even rises briefly from the dead.

The Fearless Vampire Killers, directed by Roman Polanski and starring his then-wife, Sharon Tate, is quite entertaining as a movie—and genuinely frightening in its prescience.

Heart of Darkness is loaded with vampiric overtones of the grimmest kind, all the more powerful because the story is based on Conrad's actual experience. In terms of emotional vampirism, look for the effect on the narrator, Marlowe, as expressed in a passage near the end: he speaks of returning to "the sepulchral city," and his despair, emptiness, and loathing for the life around him after what he's been through.

The Immoralist is narrated by a man who consciously allows his young wife to sicken and die, while his own suppressed wild nature grows increasingly unrestrained. Another of André Gide's creations, Lafcadio, devotes himself to the concept of unmotivated crime, such as the murder of a total stranger.

Là-bas (French; the usage in this context means "hell") is a late nineteenth-century novel by Parisian writer and occultist J. K. Huysmans. It's of particular interest because it brings occult vampirism into the realm of reality. Aspects of it are based on Huysmans's experiences with a satanist group, and it includes a biography of one of history's most grotesque vampiric murderers, Gilles de Rais.

Les Liaisons Dangereuses, in its various versions, tells the story of a team who set out systematically to ruin a young woman through seduction. The Marquise de Merteuil, the guiding force, is clearly motivated by something beyond sex, money, power (in the usual sense), or even malice.

Les Misérables exemplifies another broad group of dramas, in which the vampire is society itself. In this case, it's personified as Javert, the detective who relentlessly pursues Valjean for his theft of a loaf of bread. Variations include numerous socially conscious novels, where individuals or groups are oppressed by political/economic/societal forces (*All Quiet on the Western Front, The Grapes of Wrath, The Invisible Man, Jude the Obscure, The Jungle, Oliver Twist, The Scarlet Letter*); more abstract, psychological treatments (*Day of the Locust, Lord of the Flies, The Stranger*); and on into the realm where the predation is so amorphous and removed, it can only be dealt with through metaphor (Kafka, Cocteau, other forms of experimental and surreal writing).

Long Day's Journey into Night is probably Eugene O'Neill's best-known play, about a family plagued with ailments and addictions, tearing each other apart.

The Miracle of the Rose, Querelle (also a film, directed by Fassbinder), and other works by Jean Genet portray fierce sexual vampirism.

Naked Lunch and other works by William Burroughs portray vampirism on many levels, from the surreal to as real as it gets: heroin addiction, and the predators who inhabit that world.

Of Human Bondage tells the story of a shy young doctor's obsession with a hard-hearted, trampy waitress, who breaks him down with conscious cruelty and sexual manipulation until he's on the verge of collapse.

Othello features the most purely evil of Shakespeare's creations: Iago, whose intricate manipulations goad Othello into murdering his angelic wife.

(The Bard remains unmatched at creating villains, but most— Macbeth, Richard III—are at least partly motivated by hunger for power, women, etc. Iago seems to desire nothing of the sort. He speaks of his own "gain," but it's clearly not material; and at the end, even under threat of torture, remains silent. His final cryptic line, "what you know, you know," suggests that his secret motive was shared, if unconsciously, by Othello.)

The Picture of Dorian Gray resembles the Faustus legend and Jekyll and Hyde, in that it's primarily a metaphor for the vampiric process. The title character, a young man of great physical beauty, descends into degradation that results in murder (of the portrait's painter), but his outward appearance remains unchanged. Instead, the ravages of his soul appear on his portrait, hidden in a locked room until the moment of reckoning.

The Possessed (Dostoyevsky) portrays another most extreme creation of a writer who often went deep and dark into the human psyche. Stavrogin is not so much evil as utterly amoral; his crimes (including, in a suppressed chapter which the publishers refused to print, the rape and murder of a young girl) are committed under the guise of political anarchy, but it's clear that this is not the real motive. At the end—not remorseful, but weary, realizing he'll never fill his inner emptiness—he hangs himself.

Powaqqatsi, sequel to *Koyaanisqatsi,* is a film montage without plot or dialogue, set to powerful music by Philip Glass. The images combine to form a most unsettling look at the modern world, particularly at ravages on the poor and exploited. The title is Hopi, meaning "an entity, a way of life, that consumes life forces of other beings in order to further its own life."

The Sun Also Rises revolves around Brett, who damages every man she touches, and yet who herself emerges as a tormented, tragic figure.

Tender Is the Night is, strictly speaking, out of our bounds because of Nicole's madness, but the story is too haunting an example of psychological destruction to leave unmentioned. We'll also note *The Great Gatsby,* with Daisy and Tom characterizing a self-centered, vampiric, upper crust: careless people who broke things, and left the mess for others to clean up.

That Evening Sun is a particularly pointed example of the casual brutality and racism that pervades Faulkner's work, emblematic of cultures where a combination of societal and individual vampirism is considered to be the proper order of things. A young black woman, pregnant by a white man, dares to accost him. She's beaten, jailed, driven
to temporary madness, and attempts suicide. Finally, she's abandoned
by her white employers to be murdered by her jealous black lover. The
story is seen through the eyes of uncomprehending, playful children.

"Torch Song" is one of John Cheever's darkest stories. A New Yorker
realizes that over a period of decades, a woman he knows has been
involved with several men—all of whom have died soon after. She
doesn't murder or harm them: she's just there. Toward the end,
when he's sick and weak, she pays a call on him.

Under the Volcano revolves around the emotional havoc wrought by
the fiercely alcoholic consul. Particularly memorable is a scene
where he sets out to psychologically destroy his brother, who's
having an affair with his (the consul's) long-suffering wife.

Whatever Happened to Baby Jane? represents a kind of psychological
horror, in which a vampiric character terrorizes a victim(s)—a
family member, or other who's emotionally close and can't escape.
Similar scenarios include *The Comedian*; *Hush, Hush, Sweet Charlotte*;
Mommie, Dearest.

Who's Afraid of Virginia Woolf? is among the most chilling emotional
vampire examples of all, precisely because it's so firmly grounded in
the everyday world. Burton and Taylor are a skilled team, playing
"get the guest"—devastating a younger couple, and each other.